You Too?

EDITED BY

JANET GURTLER

ink
yard
press

ink
yard
press

Recycling programs
for this product may
not exist in your area.

ISBN-13: 978-1-335-92908-2

CONTENTS

For everyone out there who needs a hug.
I know there's a person who wants to give you one.
I hope you find each other.

You Too?

In 2018, #MeToo stories began exploding across my social media feed, bringing back memories of the harassment I experienced as a young woman coming of age in the late seventies and early eighties. In addition to big hair and terrible clothing choices, I grew up believing that the women's movement had "already happened." In North America, the Pill had become legal for single women in addition to those who were married. Many women were stepping out of the kitchen, beginning to make livings on their own. Gloria Steinem, a well-known feminist, was famously attributed with saying that women needed a man like a fish needed a bicycle (although she later clarified it was Irina Dunn who said it first). Glass ceilings for women were acknowledged and sometimes—though not often—shattered. Helen Gurely

Brown, the editor of *Cosmopolitan* magazine, wrote a book about women "Having It All," which fed the illusion that women could have it all. That they *should*.

There was also an illusion that women were finally being treated equally to men. And yet, even in spite of all this "progression," I knowingly accepted less money because of my gender, and I was perfectly okay with it. I thought I didn't deserve to ask for more. I didn't want to ruffle feathers. So I listened to sexist jokes. Racist jokes. When I was harassed, I was a good sport about it.

And I didn't speak up.

For years, I kept silent, learning to smile and play nice. But as more and more women came forward to tell their #MeToo stories, a burning fire began to ignite within me, a fire fueled by anger and empathy—until one evening, when I found myself ranting at my husband and teenage son at the dinner table, I finally realized how passionate I felt.

I told them some of the things I went through as a teenager, knowing they couldn't possibly understand the scope of what happens to women *all the time*, or why this flood of #MeToo stories made me so upset. As I shared my own stories, I discovered that my son truly believed his world was not one where women were still paid less than men. Or were harassed for being women. To him, such injustice was a part of my lifetime and his grandparents' lifetimes, something long past.

I may have scoffed at him. Perhaps not kindly.

He didn't see the truth—not because he is a bad person, or because he didn't want to see it, but because he had not been properly shown.

I knew then that I needed to do a better job. As a mother, I needed to show him the truth about the world we live in.

I needed to share my stories—and not just with my husband and son, but with anyone who would listen.

That conversation with my son made me realize I wanted to take action. I wanted to share #MeToo stories with other young people like him, so they could see where we were, and how far we still need to go to make this world a kinder, more just place for our children.

I'm not an expert; I hold no degrees in psychology or human behavior. I can't offer professional help, and I acknowledge that, as a white woman, I am speaking from a place of privilege. I am also becoming one of the older generation now, and sometimes I use outdated terms and think in old ways. I've been called out and challenged to look at the things I say and think about how my wording might marginalize some groups of people. I often make mistakes, though I am trying to do better.

But one thing I do know for certain is that we need to stand together. To protect each other. To amplify the voices of those who are so often robbed of their ability to speak. There are still many #MeToo fights to be fought—and we need to fight them together.

So I set out to collect stories from a diverse group of writers who were willing to share their personal encounters— stories that have now found a home within the pages of this book. There are a range of experiences here, though not nearly enough. There are many other stories to be heard— from women *and* men, since harassment and abuse are certainly not exclusive to females. I've heard from men who were robbed of their virginity at an early age, by other men and by women. Men who were forced into sex because their physical response to stimulation was taken as consent. Men who feared talking about what happened to them, or speaking about how much it affected and hurt them. Because they'd been taught that "men should always want sex."

We need to hear their truths, too.

As you read the stories in this book, it will become obvious that the world is not a perfect place. Sometimes adults don't do the right thing. Sometimes the people who are supposed to love us and protect us can't or don't. And sometimes, when someone tried to tell their story, others couldn't hear it. Or refused to.

Some of the contributors worried that their stories weren't enough. That what happened to them wasn't as bad as what happened to others. But I believe all these stories are important. It's not easy to go back and relive our most painful memories, and it's even harder to expose them to strangers. And yet—here we are. Sharing them with you. We have each done so for our own reasons, but mainly it's to keep important conversations going. We want to see things change. We want people to feel less alone.

We want *you* to feel less alone.

Maybe you believe you deserve the bad things that have happened to you. (You don't.) Maybe someone is blaming you. Or maybe you're too afraid to tell. Maybe it feels like your problem is too small to worry about, or too big to do anything about.

It's not.

Please know, no matter what—you are not alone.

If you have experienced harassment or abuse, you might find triggers in these pages. Rape. Incest. Exploitation. The #MeToo stories you will read here are hard, but there are people and organizations out there who care and want to help. Please use the resources included if any of these stories upset you, or if you've had similar experiences. Please reach out if you need support.

And finally, respect yourself, but please also respect the people who are brave enough to share their stories. In some ways, telling our truths is like standing naked in front of the whole world. It's intimidating and uncomfortable, and we may feel weird talking about it after.

But we need to keep talking. We need to keep listening. For that is the only way we'll be able to change the world.

—Janet

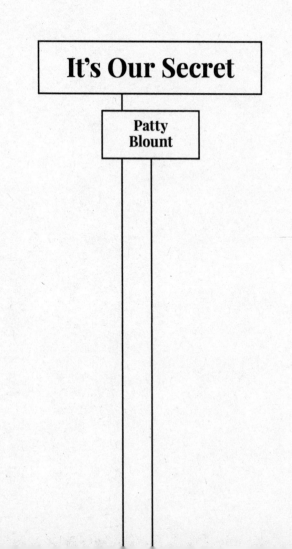

It's Our Secret

Patty
Blount

Secrets.

What word can conjure up more magic than this? Secrets are a little girl's stock and trade, guaranteed to make eyes light up with mischief or excitement. Secrets are a game you play to test the limits of trust and of loyalty. Secrets are whisper campaigns designed to include only a chosen few, and if you're one of the chosen, suddenly you're special. You're favored.

You're *it.*

Secrets are important in most little girls' lives. I think this is exactly why the neighbor told me, "It's our secret. If you tell anybody, then they'll want to play our tickle game, too. It won't be special anymore."

I was five. I wanted to be special. I wanted to be the favorite. So I didn't tell.

I didn't tell anybody that this man lay me down in the back of his work van, took my pants down, and touched me *there*. But that's not the only reason I didn't tell. I didn't tell because at age five, I had no idea this was wrong.

I grew up in the Queens neighborhood of Flushing, in a small garden apartment complex near Francis Lewis Boulevard. When I was little, we didn't have *playdates*. In the summer months, you just went outdoors after breakfast and played with whichever kids were out. We had no phones, no internet. We had bikes and imaginations and very little supervision—which meant we got into trouble often. But always the innocent kind.

I wasn't allowed to cross any streets by myself, so I had to stay on our block. Riding bicycles was the preferred activity, but sometimes, it was too hot to do that, so we'd look for shady spots.

The best shady spot was in the garages under the building. There were three of them. Three two-car garages with stairway access to a specific apartment above. One of these garages was where our neighbor kept his work van. He was a house painter, so the van always had a bunch of paint cans smeared with drips in the back. He had two sons, the oldest of whom was the same age as me.

Five.

For the most part, I liked playing with this boy I'll call Billy. He had cool toys, like the cars we could sit inside and pedal around the garage, pretending we were racing. Billy also had a great imagination. He'd frequently make up games we could play, like monster tag. One day, when we were playing house, he said I should ask his dad to make my doll a cradle out of a box we found that was just the right size for a baby bed. So that's what I did. I took the box and the doll and went to the van where Billy's dad was loading those drippy paint cans. His clothes and hands were splattered with paint, too.

I asked him if he could make a doll bed out of the box, and he said, "Sure. But first, I want to play with you, okay?"

Play with me? Sure! I nodded happily.

"But it's a secret," he said. "You can't tell anybody, or they'll want to play, too."

A secret? Oh, boy!

He picked me up, set me on the floor of the van, pushed me back, and took off my pants. They were shorts, actually. I could even tell you what color, but that's not important. He had a cigarette clamped in the corner of his mouth as he put his hand between my legs and rubbed.

"Does that tickle? Does that feel good?" he asked.

I wasn't entirely sure if it tickled or felt good. I was too busy thinking about the doll bed he was going to make me. After what felt like a long time passed, I said, "Can I go play house with Billy now?"

He gave me a little pat on my leg, put my clothes back where they belonged, and lifted me up. "Remember, you can't tell anybody. This is our secret."

Then he took out a tool from his pocket and began slicing through the cardboard box I'd given him, shaping it into the perfect bed for my doll.

I was five.

I can't remember how many times this happened. And I can't answer this one burning question that still haunts me: Did his son know? Did Billy send me to his father, knowing what he'd do to me? Was he a victim, as well? Does he remember?

I remember eventually seeing a pediatrician because it hurt

every time I peed. I had an infection and had to take medicine that looked like M&M's and turned my pee orange.

Still, I kept the secret. I can't remember how long. But, as I said, secrets are a form of currency to little girls. One night, when my mother wasn't paying enough attention to me, I sang, "I've got a secret and I'm not telling."

Oh, boy, did that get her attention.

So I told her all about the van and the paint and the tickle game, and that it was supposed to be a secret.

She went completely still. She asked me to say it again. And again. For a moment, I worried I'd done something wrong. That telling my secret was wrong. Then my mother told me *keeping* the secret was what was wrong, but I didn't understand why.

Finally, my mother collected herself and tucked me into bed, and I fell asleep, content once more—until later that night, when she woke me up and took me to the living room.

There were several men waiting for us. Men I'd never seen before—and Billy's dad. He stood just inside the door, arms folded across his chest, scowl on his face. My mother said I had to tell the men in the living room everything I told her about the tickle game secret. I did, but I think I spent more time talking about the doll bed Billy's dad had made for me.

Nobody laughed. Nobody even smiled.

One of those men asked, "Are you lying? Are you pretending?"

I shook my head and turned to Billy's dad, hoping he'd back me up. I didn't understand this was bad. I didn't know that *he'd* lie.

I was five.

He lied.

My mother told me to go back to bed. I obeyed, but stayed

awake for a long time. I was crushed by the things I'd heard in that living room. He told them I bothered him. That I kept playing with his tools and his paint, and he'd threatened to spank me if I didn't get lost.

That never happened.

He lied.

Later, there were lots of whispered arguments between my parents. I couldn't hear most of it. But I did hear this: "Why was she playing in those garages in the first place?"

I remember baths. Lots of baths, where I was scrubbed raw.

There were many looks aimed at me—looks of accusation, blame, and even disgust. I felt wrong. Guilty. I'd told my secret.

And he lied.

Billy and his family moved away in the middle of the night.

"You play right here where I can see you," my mother said after.

"But I want to ride my bike."

"No. You stay right here, or you go to your room."

So I stayed right in front of the door, bored out of my mind. Every time I went to the bathroom, she followed me, looked inside the bowl.

My pee was orange for a long time.

A few weeks later, I was playing with other friends while our moms chatted. One of the boys said, "Let's play hide-and-seek." Enthusiastically, I agreed. He began counting. I ran down the steps to the garage under the building, which was full of great hiding places.

My mother chased me, demanded I never go down to the garage again.

Our game of hide-and-seek never even got started. Brian,

the boy who'd suggested it, wanted to know why we couldn't play in the garage anymore. His mom and my mom exchanged a glance. You know the one. It's a look that says, "I have no idea how to explain this."

So they didn't.

But I did.

I told Brian, "They're mad at Billy's dad for tickling me down there." I pointed between my legs, and both moms nearly passed out. Brian suddenly had to go home, and I was once again stuck in my room.

"You can't tell people about this. Ever," my mother said. "Billy's dad did a bad thing. A very bad thing. We shouldn't talk about it, because everyone will think it's your fault if you do."

That made no sense to me, but I listened. I didn't talk about the tickle game. I didn't play as much as I used to. I never went down to the garages.

I don't remember exactly when I learned that those men who came to see me were detectives. And I don't remember exactly when I realized that what happened wasn't just *bad*— it was unspeakable.

Eventually I began to understand. The word *molested* entered my vocabulary. I learned that the two detectives in our living room that night advised my parents not to press charges because I would then be made to testify, to tell a judge what Billy's father did. And because he lied, because he said it was just my imagination, the judge would probably believe him instead of me. So they opted to spare me the ordeal.

Or were they just sparing themselves?

Despite everything, I grew up fairly normal, except I now have this terrible aversion to the smell of house paint and cigarettes, and a morbid fear of vans. I sometimes wonder how many other secrets Billy's father had. How many other kids did he molest? It's a hard question to answer, because his crime is so unspeakable, but now, I find myself troubled by an even harder question that we've never dared to ask aloud:

How many kids could we have spared if we hadn't kept it a secret?

★ ★ ★ ★ ★

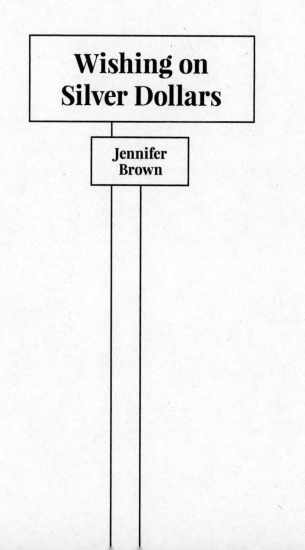

Wishing on
Silver Dollars

Jennifer
Brown

"Wow, I'll bet your nipples are as big as silver dollars!" Michael proclaimed as he stood behind me in line at the diving board. He was not at all original in subject choice. By that time—at the ripe old age of barely thirteen—I had heard it all. *I'll bet if you drop your pencil at your neck, it never hits the ground. I'll bet you could use those tits as a table. I'll bet you don't know what your feet look like.* Or, even more embarrassingly, *I'll bet you can't even see your...* Well, you know where that's going.

It wasn't only the swimming pool where I had to duck and dodge boys like Michael. The hallways in my junior high school during passing period were some of the most naked fully-clothed moments of my life. Boys' overtly sexual comments—often accompanied by "accidental" brushes, grabs, and gropes—were often the burden of early-developing girls like me. It was a captive environment where neither fight nor flight seemed like a viable option. Our only choices were to wish we could crawl into a hole or wish they would fall into a hole or maybe the entire school would crumble into a hole—whatever it took to make it just stop happening.

Maybe they were embarrassed by their own bodies and unattainable fantasies, or maybe they were looking to divert attention from themselves. Or maybe boys like Michael—who would publicly and loudly undress us, and deem us fit or unfit to be the subjects of a multitude of sexual acts—were just plain mean. Whatever their reasons, they passed the embarrassment on to us—a burdensome backpack to carry to our next class and frantically try to empty before diving out into those hallways again in an hour. Knowing that in an hour, Michael, or one of his dozens of stand-ins, would be waiting to mentally and verbally undress us again.

At least Michael was creative, I guess. He does remain the one and only person in my life to compare my body to currency (which is interesting in that it adds actual monetary value to my sexuality, which is a concept loaded for psychoanalytical review, but that's probably an essay for another day). His English teacher might have even been tempted to give him extra points for his use of simile in casual conversation. *Comparison using* like *or as? A+, Michael!*

Except we hadn't been conversing. We weren't even friends. At the pool that day, I'd just been waiting in line for the diving board, and he just happened to be behind me. Well, he didn't *just happen to be behind me*—he just happened to be behind me, and also thinking of how he could embarrass me in a sexually "hilarious" way.

Comparison using like *or as in a degrading and humiliating, not to mention completely unnecessary, comment just to get attention and pervy laughs from your buddies? Points deducted, Michael! You fail!*

I was—and still am—a curvy girl. And while Michael's comment was far from the first comment I'd heard about my body, it would also be far from the last. In fact, he was ushering in what would become years of torment—teasing, bullying, intimidation, and unwanted touching. I was kind of shy, and definitely sexually unaware, and the attention that was repeatedly brought to my body and what someone built like me would surely want to do with it filled me with a profound shame.

Shame. Fear that *I* had done something wrong. Fear that the people closest to me would find out what kids were saying to and about me. Fear that people would think less of me. Shame that is still my companion when I reminisce about "the good old days" (which I don't often do, because they were not good—just super old).

Shame is a mystifying and powerful beast. It's the natural by-product of harassment. It's also the natural by-product of bullying. Together, they are a one-two shame punch right in the temple. *You developed early? You don't fight back? Easy opponent! TKO!* Even if your harasser eventually develops a conscience and feels responsibility for what they've done—they are only sharing the shame, not taking it from you. You own it now. It is part of you.

Shame over being harassed is also ridiculous, because I shouldn't have been ashamed of being a victim. Like *nasty woman*, I've been told, we should be proud to carry the label *slut*. I get the concept. I get the desire to take the power away from the insult by being happy to have it. But by gleefully accepting the "gift" of a label of any kind, aren't we still defining ourselves by our labeler's terms? Why should we change our paradigm to fit theirs, even if by "fit" we mean "counteract"? In doing so, we continue to give the power to our harassers. We continue to excuse their behavior by altering ours. Just because we say we're okay doesn't mean what they've done is okay.

I shouldn't have been ashamed of my body. I shouldn't have been put in situations that made me feel less-than just because other people felt the need to comment on me and my body in a sexual manner. And I especially shouldn't have been made to feel as though somehow I'd brought it on myself—that I'd wanted it, "asked for it."

You did this to yourself, curvy girl, by…uh…hmm…well, I guess by allowing nature to happen?

As a curvy girl… Actually, as a girl, period, your body is up for grabs. Sometimes literally. Too many times verbally. What you must look like naked, what you must be willing to do, what you must be able to do are all subjects open for debate. You are leered at and laughed at, and cut down for having no sense of humor if you react negatively. You are propositioned and suggested to. Your ass is smacked and nobody is the culprit, books are knocked out of your hands in hopes that your shirt will gape when you bend over to pick them up. You're reported to be into kinks you've never even heard of. Your breasts are drive-by tweaked and grazed. You are desirable in a horrible way and expected to take that as a compliment. You can never trust if a boy is into you because he genuinely likes you, or if he's into you because he likes the idea of being able to tell people he got a handful of you. You can never trust walking in a crowd. You can never trust…

Well, you can never trust. You are simply a collection of parts, just hoping to get from destination to destination with a little bit of pride intact.

When we think about sexual harassment, we may immediately conjure an image of the stereotypical lecherous executive withholding jobs and raises and corner offices until someone gets on her knees under his desk. We may think about "trading sexual favors for equality" (not true, by the way—the actual trade is favors for silence—there is nothing equal about it).

But here's the thing. When you're mentally and verbally stripped, the "favors" turn into "expectations." By God, they own the rights to those silver dollars, because they saw them first! Try to hold on to them yourself—try to defend from groping hands and groping words—and you become A Bitch. And *nobody* likes A Bitch (*tsk tsk*).

From the moment puberty kicks in, we are taught by our little peer society that our bodies don't belong to us. That we don't have a right to self-respect. We are examined and evaluated and boiled down to things and pieces and acts. And we turn on each other.

Everyone, keep looking at the well-developed girl in the corner, so you don't notice my *body. Sorry, well-developed girl in the corner, I feel bad for you—I really do!—but I don't want to become you. I've got to look out for myself.*

I'm not actually much of a fighter. And back then, I was easily intimidated. I didn't want to make people mad at me. So I smiled—even laughed—at jokes that degraded me! Said nothing, did nothing to protect myself. I even tried to see them as compliments—maybe not exactly the compliment I was looking for, but beggars can't be choosers, you know. I absorbed the torment, so I didn't anger my tormentors. I knew that doing so would only ramp up the harassment, as they got even more followers on their side.

All aboard the Harassment Train! First stop, Girl with Big Boobs and a Bad Attitude! Second stop, Girl Who Sleeps Around (we know it's true because, I mean, look at that ass!)! Third stop, Girl Who Wears Too-Tight Clothing! Fourth stop, Girl Who Wouldn't Put Up with It If She Didn't Secretly Like It! Fifth stop, Girl I'll Pretend to Be Falling in Love with Until I Find Out She Won't Sleep with Me! Sixth stop, Girl Who Will Take My Compliment as a Compliment If She Knows What's Good for Her, Because I'm Popular and She's Not and I Will Devastate Her Life If She Doesn't!

The saddest thing is, my story isn't unique. I shudder to think how many of us are desperately yanking at the emergency stop lever to get off the Harassment Train, all while laughing at the jokes, ignoring the grabs, pretending it's okay because sticks and stones and all that rot (what a bullshit saying that is). How many of us have so many #MeToo stories, we have trouble choosing which one to talk about? How many of us never talk at all, because #MeToo has an ugly hashtag twin: #ShameToo?

By the time we even reach the point of vying for careers, we have lived with harassment for so long, we forget that it's there. We overlook it and ignore it and laugh along with it, and then carry our shame like an extra appendage and ask ourselves what we could have done differently to keep that from happening to us next time. Because if we know one thing for sure, we know there *will* be a next time. We have already spent our entire puberty under the thumbs of our "superiors," understanding that if we want to survive in our social structure, we must smile prettily, and act flattered that someone noticed us. We must happily accept our "riches," one silver dollar at a time.

Shame runs deep, but it also runs long. I don't like to talk about that time of my life because I don't like to think about it. I'm still carrying that damn backpack, and I will never dig out the ugliest items that have fallen to the bottom. It's just way too deep, and my arms are too short, and I can't reach them. I wish I could go back in time and walk those junior high hallways with my thirteen-year-old self. I wish I could counsel her. I would tell her:

You are not a collection of body parts. You do not have to put up with people saying that you are. You do not have to laugh along, or stay silent, or worry that you are doing something wrong. You have a right to sexual privacy. You have a right to body privacy. Dammit, you have a right to privacy!

Back then, I wished someone had told me not to wear that particular swimsuit to the public pool. Which was silly, because the one-piece swimsuit showed absolutely nothing, and even if I had been wearing a wool turtleneck to the pool, Michael still would have "seen" those silver dollars. It wasn't about something I wore or something I did. It just wasn't.

Now, I wish something very different. I wish I hadn't felt like I had done something wrong by wearing the wrong thing. I wish I hadn't decided that his mortifying comment was my fault; something I had brought upon myself. I wish I hadn't felt like somehow I had done something that made it okay for a boy to loudly and publicly assess what my naked body might look like. I wish I hadn't just accepted that these kinds of comments were a girl's burden to bear. I wish I had refused to shoulder that backpack.

More than anything, I wish someone had taught Michael better.

★ ★ ★ ★ ★

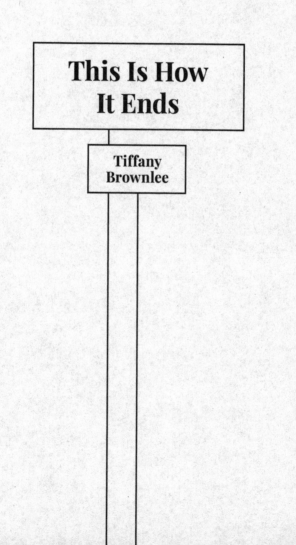

This Is How It Ends

Tiffany
Brownlee

I wish I could say that there was never a time in my life where I felt out of place or unwanted because of my race, but unfortunately for me (and many other people of color, I'm sure), that's not the case. I also wish I could say that I've never been sexually assaulted by someone, but again, for me and far too many girls and women around the world, that is not the case.

My story starts in San Diego, California—my birthplace and hometown. I'm not sure if you're aware of how many—few—Black people lived in San Diego in the '90s and early 2000s, but to put it in perspective, let's just say that in all my elementary classes of twenty-five to twenty-eight students, I was either the only Black kid in the class or one of two or three. There weren't many of us, but as a child, that had absolutely no effect on how I felt about myself. As far as I was concerned, that was the norm, and I never questioned it.

Except for one time when my mother was doing my hair.

"Mom," I said as she twisted my hair into a poufy spiral and clamped a colorful clip on the ends to keep them from unraveling, "why don't I have hair like my doll?" Sitting snugly on a pink stool between her legs, I turned for her to finish the other side of my head, and I showed her my Barbie doll. "See," I said, running my fingers through the doll's head of platinum blond hair. "Her hair is so pretty and mine's so... nappy." I wanted to say ugly, but deep down I knew I didn't have ugly hair. Just different hair. "I never even have to comb Barbie's hair to get it soft or straight. It's just always like that."

"Oh, Tiffany." She frowned. "You have pretty hair, too. Just like your dolls."

"Then why don't they make a lot of Barbies with skin and hair like mine? All of my friends have hair like Barbie's, and all of my Barbies have hair like them. I'm the only one who doesn't." Even at eight years old, I was more woke to the underrepresentation of Black culture in the real world than many people are today.

"Just...because, Tiffany," was her reply. That's what she always said when she didn't have the answer to something, or when it was too deep a concept for me to fully grasp. I'm sure that "just because" bothered her more than she let on, but I was young. Too young to understand the realness lying just under the surface of that conversation.

It's not that I was in denial about being different as I was growing up. I was very aware of the distinct differences between me and my White neighbors across the street or my Filipino neighbors next door. Yes, I was different, but the beauty of living in San Diego was that about half of the population was just like me: a minority. So, even though I was (for the most part) the lone Black girl in my classes at school, I wasn't alone in feeling that way. There were probably plenty of other young girls of color asking their mothers the same question about Barbies as I was.

In fact, the lack of other Black people in my area gave me the opportunity to make friends with so many children of other races. I had White friends, Black friends, Asian friends, Hispanic/Latino friends, Indian friends… I mean, the list could go on and on. And the cool thing was that even though we came from different places and had different facial features and spoke with different dialects and accents, we were friends. We liked to play on the jungle gym after school each day and visit the beach on weekends. I was just like them, and they were just like me.

And then, in the middle of my sixth-grade year, my parents sat me and my siblings down to tell us something huge: We. Were. Moving.

My dad was in the military, so I was used to moving around, but this was a different kind of relocation, and they made sure to clarify that: we were moving OUT OF STATE, to New Orleans, Louisiana.

On the outside, I acted as if I was as cool as a cucumber, but on the inside, I was angry and confused and sad. I'd lived in California my entire life, so relocating to "The Boot State," as I called it, was an earth-shattering revelation. My parents wanted me to be excited with them, but I couldn't bring myself to do it. I already had a lot on my plate: I was waiting for my womanly body parts to arrive, preparing for my first visit from "Aunt Flow," and figuring out how to increase my popularity status for the next year, which involved joining several sports teams. I didn't have the mental capacity to focus on yet another move when there were so many other things going on inside of me.

I put on a smile anyway. The decision had already been made, and nothing I said or did was going to change that.

I was hit with a ton of major cultural changes when we arrived in New Orleans. The biggest change was that I went from being part of a minority race on the West Coast to being part of the majority in the South. For the first time, I was surrounded by tons of people who looked like me and had the potential to understand the challenges that came along with being Black. In California, few people understood my curly hair and the fact that I didn't get sunburned when I spent more than fifteen minutes outside in direct sunlight. So while I missed California with all my heart, it was nice to be around people who shared similarities with me. People who understood me.

My joy of being surrounded by people who looked like me was short-lived, though. When school started, reality hit. Hard.

Because of my grades at my previous school, I was placed in a combination of regular education classes and honors classes. I was elated to be in the honors classes in Louisiana, but when I walked in on my first day, my excitement faded. Again, I was the only Black student in those classes. I can still feel the chills crawling up my back and the knots forming in my stomach when I strolled across the classroom to take my seat for the first time. The stares from the other kids in the class said it all: "Why is a Black kid taking honors?"

Things didn't get any better in my regular education classes, either. Some of the Black kids in my classes turned up their noses at me and snickered to their friends as I walked by. Whenever I'd answer a question in class, they'd mock me, mimicking my speech pattern because I enunciated every sound and syllable perfectly and properly. I didn't understand it. I couldn't wrap my head around what their problem was with me.

At lunch a few weeks later, I finally found out why they treated me as if I was an outcast, even though we both had the same shade of honey-brown skin. After paying for my tray of food, I hesitated before choosing a seat. I hadn't made any real friends yet and was still sitting wherever there was an open spot at the time. That day, I tried to sit next to a group of Black girls. As I put my tray down, a girl from the group tried to push it off the table.

"Sorry," she said with a smirk, "this seat's taken."

I was young and new to interpreting tone of voice and body language, so bravely I asked, "Oh, sorry. Who's sitting here?"

"Anyone but you, White girl. Find another seat." She turned back to her friends, who all simultaneously mimed flipping their hair over their shoulders before they burst into laughter. I didn't understand the joke, and I stood there awhile longer, my food growing colder as I tried to figure it all out. Eventually, the girl turned back, rolling her eyes, and pushed my tray away from the table for the second time.

"Look, I'm only gonna say this once, White girl," she said, leaning in closer to me, her brown eyes locking on mine with a rich intensity. "We don't want you here. You may look like us, but you will never act like us. And I don't care where you go, but you can take your wannabe-White ass and sit somewhere else."

I headed to another table to eat, this one filled with mainly White students. But as I set my tray down, one of the boys at the table turned to me and pursed his lips in a disapproving way.

"Hey," he said, "don't think that just because they don't want you that we do. Dr. King Jr. may have made it okay for you to go to school with us with his speech, but nothing's changed, nigger. Find another table."

That word. To this day, that word burns a hole in my heart. Hearing it that day marked the first time I was ever made to feel inferior to another race. Yes, the Barbie conversation with my mom hinted at the idea that we, as a Black race, were inferior to White people—the fact that society expected me to play with a doll that didn't represent what I looked like on the outside was a flashing neon sign foreshadowing the hidden racism I would have to endure as I grew older—but it wasn't until I heard someone call me a nigger that I actually felt like less of a person, just because I was born with a little more melanin in my skin than some people would have liked.

In that moment, I realized I was seriously on my own. Neither the White kids nor the Black kids at my school wanted anything to do with me, for no good reason at all. And as a kid who was so open and accepting of other races and people of different backgrounds (because that's how I was raised to be), I was completely blown away by their actions. *What's so wrong with me?* I thought to myself, but what I should have been asking was, *What's wrong with them?* and *Who taught them to see one race as superior to another?*

Sometimes, I look back, and I want to kick myself. Maybe I should have given them a piece of my mind, but I wasn't the kind of person who was comfortable verbalizing my feelings of hurt or disappointment. So, rather than tell someone—a teacher, the counselor, my parents, anyone—about the conversations I'd had with the students that day, I internalized it. They didn't want me around them, and so I tried my hardest to disappear. I stopped speaking up in my classes even when I knew the right answers, I sat alone during lunch, and I stayed out of everyone's way. Essentially, I made myself invisible to make them more comfortable, and looking back on the situation, that was absolutely not okay.

Their words stuck with me, and it wasn't until the end of eighth grade that I met a friend who started to help me come to terms with being confident in the brown skin I was in. Vee was a biracial girl who'd moved to New Orleans from Washington. She was extremely intelligent, and was placed in the honors classes, too. And like me, she was treated as if she was less-than by the other students at our school. She was shunned by the Black community, who said she was a mutt—that her White side made her too White to hang out with them—and outcasted by the White kids, who didn't believe she, as a half-Black person, was smart enough to be in the honors classes.

One day, when we ended up at the same lunch table, I gathered up enough nerve to ask her if she was bothered by the way the other students at our school treated her.

"Why should I be?" she questioned me. "It's them who have the problem, because as far as I'm concerned there's only one race, and that's human."

Her coolness was inspiring, but it wasn't exactly what I was looking for. I wanted a fix-all of sorts. Something that I could use instantly to make the situation better. But that wasn't what I got, so I pocketed her thoughts on the matter and set out to bridge the racial divide. I struggled through the remainder of my middle school days, but things got a little better in high school. Better, however, doesn't necessarily mean my issues were completely resolved.

With a larger population at my high school, I began to see more diversity in my honors classes, and just like Vee, the

Black students in my classes seemed so sure of themselves. I craved that security, and I envied them for finding it before I did. I thought if I could feign that confidence, then maybe I'd be happier. It took a while for people to notice, but after a few weeks, I began to see a change in the way the White students handled my Black presence in the honors classes. I was no longer getting comments from the White kids that made me feel as if I didn't belong there; in fact, they welcomed me to the class and made a point to include me in their lives inside and outside of school. I wasn't made fun of by the Black kids because I "acted White" and "talked White," like I was back in middle school. Yes, there were still people who snuck an occasional racist comment into conversation (and I learned to keep my distance from those people), but for the most part, the racial issues I'd experienced in middle school were essentially nonexistent in high school. Still, I wanted to fit in even more, which brings me to the next part of my story.

By the middle of my sophomore year, I'd come to be accepted among my peers and classmates, but I still wasn't fitting in, per se. I didn't have an arsenal of high school friends like MTV's *Laguna Beach* led me to believe I would have, but I had a few good ones. It wasn't much, but it was enough.

This, however, didn't sit well with my mom, and it's most likely the reason she asked her friend's daughter—Shay—to invite me to her school dance. I didn't even want to go at first. I mean, how sad was I that my mom had to ask her colleagues if I could tag along to their daughters' school activities? Somehow, though, they convinced me to go, and so I did. Shay was a nice-enough person, and despite the fact that this was all a setup, it sounded like fun. *What could go wrong?* I thought.

When we got there, it was like night and day compared to

the dances I'd been to before. My school dances were spacious, the music was kept at a conservative volume, and there were tons of staff members present to avoid any raunchy dancing or heavy make-out sessions. But at Shay's school, the room was packed wall-to-wall with people, the music was turned up as high as it could go, and from what I could tell, there were no chaperones at all. I didn't know it at the time, but this was all setting me up for a moment I'd never forget. A moment that'd stay with me well into my adulthood.

I was a dancer and therefore used to classical ballet, tap, and jazz, so the twerking (or "booty popping" and "grinding," as I called it back then) the other students were doing at the dance threw me for a loop. I didn't want this to be another instance where I stood out or didn't fit in, so I asked Shay to teach me how to do it, and she did.

"Put your hands on your knees and lean forward," she instructed, "and arch and un-arch your back really fast. Guys will come up to dance behind you if you're good." I'm sure I looked awkward at first, but I got the hang of it eventually, and before I knew it, boys whose names I didn't even know were coming over to dance with me. They'd grab my waist and pull me closer and press their bodies up against mine. I loved every second of the attention I got from them. Guys at my school never even gave me a second glance, but here, I was wanted. Here, I was fitting in, I was making friends, I was the girl I'd always wanted to be.

The feeling was fleeting, though, for when I took a break from dancing to visit the girls' restroom, I learned the truth behind the attention I'd been receiving on the dance floor. Shay pulled me away from the mirror, where I'd been applying another coat of lip gloss, her eyes suddenly serious.

"Some of the girls said that you've been letting guys…*you*

know...while dancing with you." As she spoke, I noticed an audience forming behind her, half eavesdropping and half checking their hair in the mirror. I was fifteen, and I'd grown up in a pretty sheltered household, so I had to ask her to explain what she meant by "you know." Clearly, she hadn't meant sex, because I'd taken Sex Ed in sixth grade, and I knew what that involved. As far as I was concerned, I'd been dancing with those guys, and nothing more. But apparently, it was much more than that.

As Shay put it, the guys were pulling out their penises and putting them on my butt and back as we danced. Whenever I'd satisfied them enough to reach their climax, they'd spray their secretions on my back and leave, making room for the next guy to dance with me. The cycle repeated, one guy after another for an entire hour, and I'd been unaware of it the entire time.

"Too White to know any better," one of the girls said with a laugh as she washed her hands. And just like that, the night was ruined. My attempt to fit in had pushed me back into my corner of insecurity. It was like middle school all over again, but worse. I felt ashamed and confused, but above all I felt gross. Violated. But I couldn't let them know that. I thought it better for them to slut-shame me than see how upset I was about the entire event.

Laughing with them at my own expense, I brushed it off as if it were no big deal. But it was. At the start of the night, I was naive and innocent. Just a teenage girl looking for a night of fun and dancing. But within an hour, all those values had been stolen from me, solely because I wanted to fit in.

When I returned to the dance floor, I sat out the rest of the night and counted down the minutes until I could go home and take a shower to wash the shame from my body. I considered my actions and tried to pinpoint the specific decision that led to the night slipping away from me. The exact moment where I took a detour down a dark pathway. I ran through every minute of the evening, and every time, no matter how much I wanted to blame the boys and their lack of self-control, I ended up pointing the finger at myself. I concluded that my outfit—hip-hugger jeans and a tight-fitting tank top—and my dance moves practically begged those guys to do that to me, and it wasn't until much later that I realized how wrong I was.

This epiphany came a year or so later, right after my history teacher voiced his outrage that Obama—a Black man—had been elected president. It was then that Vee's words floated back to me. *It's them who have the problem*, she'd said at the lunch table. Up until that point, those words had applied only to my being discriminated against because of my race, but now it meant something entirely different. We, the victims of unsolicited sexual advances, were not the ones with the problem. We weren't the ones who needed to change, and we will *never* be the ones at fault when things like this happen.

This isn't a piece of my past that I've shared with many people, and it's something that I've sort of repressed over the years, mostly because I was unsure how to feel about it. But now that I'm a teacher, I see my past as a way to prevent things like this from happening in the future. Discrimination and sexual assault stem from ignorance and/or a lack of care for others around us, and it's something that can be avoided by having respect for others, by having self-control, and by having enough sense to know that just because an opportunity presents itself doesn't mean that it's okay to take advantage of someone weaker or more ignorant than you—be it physically, verbally, and/or sexually.

When I see a teachable moment in my classroom, I usually leave out the dark details of my own childhood and teenage experiences. My students don't need to know my story; what's most important are the life lessons I'm trying to get across to them. Because while making sure they do well on their end-of-year standardized tests is important, I also think educating them about how to be a good person and how to distinguish right from wrong is just as crucial to their education. I teach my students to, above all, respect themselves (that is, to love the skin they're in), respect others in the same way they do themselves, and to always, *always* "respect the bubble." Passing on these lessons helps me come to terms with what I didn't do about racial and sexual harassment when I was their age.

Because books like this one and conversations like the ones I have with my students are how we can break the vicious cycle of sexual assault and racism in this world. This is how it starts, and this is how it ends.

★ ★ ★ ★ ★

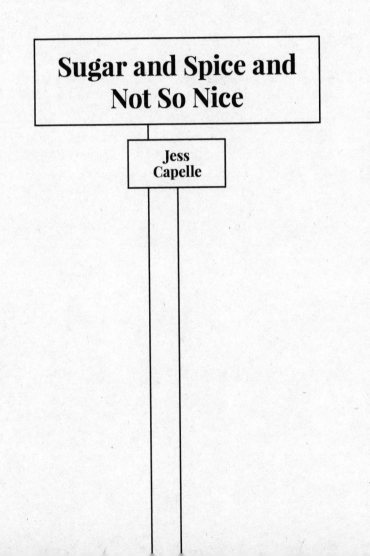

Sugar and Spice and Not So Nice

Jess Capelle

Growing up, the idea of being a "good girl" was spoon-fed to us like medicine, with a wink and a smile like so much sugar to get it down. Good girls made people feel comfortable. They did what they were told and didn't upset anyone. Good girls respected their elders, too. So, we kept our mouths shut and remained polite, even when adults said or did something that made us uncomfortable.

A lot of things adults did and said made me uncomfortable. Misogyny and sexism seemed a part of almost every interaction. As I got older, I cringed at the constant comments men made about women's bodies, their obsession with breasts, and the derogatory terms they used to talk about women. It bothered me that men didn't seem to listen to and respect women's opinions and that television and books reinforced that message, reducing women to unattractive stereotypes. If you showed off your body, you were judged. If you covered it up, you were judged in a different way.

I saw the hypocrisy.

I eventually came to understand that the female body was like a loaded weapon. You could wave it around to get what you wanted, or hide it, but either way, it made you a target for people looking to use it. That lesson sank in early and was repeated frequently enough that it shaped my life in ways I can't completely quantify. It wasn't until I started writing and thinking about the impact of my own words as an adult that I realized just how deeply those early messages had taken up residence in my brain. Little girls were supposed to be sugar and spice and everything nice. Then they were supposed to grow up to be women who remained polite and made people comfortable, even while men behaved in the worst ways possible.

In the photo album of my life, among so many blurry, out-of-focus images, a few remain as clear as if projected onto a movie screen. So many of those are memories of men behaving badly while people told me to be polite and not make waves. And as an adult, that "good girl" message still plays in my head every time I open my mouth to speak about the treatment of women.

My friends and I worshipped at the altar of author Judy Blume. Reading *Are You There God? It's Me, Margaret* changed my life. Like Margaret, I couldn't wait to get my first period and kiss a boy at a party. During sleepovers, we did exercises to increase our chest size, like Margaret did. For us, the book became a "how-to" manual for puberty.

So, when my grandmother finally informed me that we

should go shopping for a bra, I couldn't stop smiling. It signi-
fied becoming a woman, and I wanted nothing in the world
more than that. As a kid, I spent most of my time around
adults or in my own head, so I idolized my young mother and
her friends. Their lifestyle seemed so glamorous to me: driving with the windows down, listening to disco, and dancing
in clubs after leaving their office jobs.

Wearing a bra made me feel mature, strong. It made me
feel like I wasn't a child. Like I deserved respect.

Then a boy came along and changed everything.

I don't remember his name now. Brad, Chad, something
generic like that. What I do remember is that every day of
fifth grade, he tormented me in some way. He snuck up behind me and pulled my hair. Sometimes he undid the braids
or loosened my pigtails. He pushed me down or tripped me
during recess. The sidewalk surface scraped my skin each
time I fell.

He came up with insulting names for me, too. "Uncle Jesse"
was his favorite. The TV show *The Dukes of Hazzard* was big
then, and what better way to insult a girl than likening her
to an old man?

The first time he pushed me, I cried. My teacher asked
what was wrong, and I explained how he had pushed me
down, hard. She gave me a sweet smile and told me it was
just because he liked me. That was a popular explanation
back then, usually accompanied by a shrug. He liked me, so
he tormented me. Never mind the awful message about abusive behavior that sent to a whole generation of girls. When
I protested, my teacher suggested I smile and not show him
it bothered me. She said he'd stop eventually. She might as
well have said, "Be polite."

So, I did what she said, but it didn't work. In fact, my attempts to ignore him only escalated his behavior. When the usual taunts didn't make me upset, he turned to other things. Eventually, he found something particularly effective at causing a reaction, and it became his preferred tactic: snapping my bra.

My body can still recall the sting of the bra band as it smacked against my skin for the first time of many. The sharp pain traveled all the way up to my face, as if I'd been slapped. Heat bloomed there, causing me to blush and stammer. When I went to the teacher that time, she turned it around on me, like I was to blame. If I stayed away from him, he wouldn't bother me. If I hadn't encouraged him somehow, he wouldn't like me.

I got the message loud and clear. Don't make people uncomfortable. Be polite. Be a good girl.

All of my excitement at getting a bra vanished. He had weaponized the very thing that made me feel like a young woman. He had weaponized part of who I was.

Developing breasts early carried a stigma already. They brought unwanted attention from boys and jealousy from other girls. They brought body image issues. All of that would have been bad enough, but by targeting my body for his harassment, Brad—or Chad, or whatever his unmemorable name was—made me feel bad about being a girl.

With each bra snap, shame washed over me, as if I'd done something wrong, as if I were to blame. It was my fault for growing up too fast. I brought it on myself. The physical pain and the shame I felt made me angry at myself. I began to loathe my breasts, to loathe my body.

It wasn't all his fault, of course. He just served as the catalyst. He was the first one to make me a target because of my body. He was also the first one to show me how that weapon I carried around could be used most effectively against myself.

At fifteen, I took a job in a pizza place. My manager was older than me; eighteen or nineteen. He flirted with me, and I liked it, though I'm not sure if I fell more for him or for the *idea* of him. What girl didn't want an older guy?

I wasn't ready for sex, and he never pushed. But the knowledge that he'd expect it soon—he was older, after all—loomed over me like a storm cloud. Oddly, I didn't feel that weird about him being my boss, but his age bothered me when I thought too hard about it. No matter how mature I thought I was, someone who was already an adult was too old for me. It didn't help that my stepdad was twenty-nine at the time. Way too close for comfort.

So, I moved on from him, and shortly after from the pizza place. It was hard to work with my ex, and I was tired of feeling covered in grease all the time. I took a job at a grocery store instead.

My uniform consisted of a button-down shirt and pin-striped pants with matching apron. It was good quality, but the button-down was a little tight around my chest. The apron covered it well, but that didn't stop me from constantly feeling the need to adjust it. The dress code also required black work shoes, so my mom took me to buy some nice ones. They felt like standing on clouds when I tried them on. I mostly liked wearing the uniform; it made me feel more professional, despite being ill-fitting.

I learned all the ins and outs of being a cashier and easily passed the tests. Who knew that knowing the difference between cilantro and parsley would get me a job? Eager to learn any tips for making a good impression, I chatted up one of the older cashiers. As we talked, I learned I had already made an impression of a different kind.

She asked if a certain manager had hired me, and I nodded. "Figured," she said. "You can always tell. He picks 'em by bra size." Her words came out with no bitterness or anger. Just that matter-of-fact way of stating something everyone knows to be true.

I had no idea how to respond to that.

Before I'd really processed her words, she leaned in and whispered, "Listen, sweetie. Just go along with it. Flirt a little, so he feels wanted."

"But—" I barely got the word out before she jumped back in.

"Oh no, honey, he won't hurt cha or anything. He'll just give you the best shifts."

The snapshot of that conversation hasn't faded, even though her name did long ago. I remember thinking she had to be wrong, but I didn't want to be rude and call her on it. Memory is a funny thing, especially when it comes to harassment. In the moment, you feel like you're misinterpreting. You want to give the benefit of the doubt. You want to maintain the status quo and be polite. Later, you see it clearly for what it was, but that doesn't keep you from questioning yourself and how bad it actually was.

After my conversation with my coworker, I second-guessed everything. Had I really been hired only because of my breasts? Would I lose my job if I didn't flirt with him? I became constantly aware of my body and wished I could make myself invisible. I cursed Judy Blume for making me hope for larger breasts as a kid.

Because now, my breasts were a weapon again. Causing me difficulties, making me a target.

The hiring manager watched me while I worked. Sizing me up to see if I would play along, I guessed. He was always polite and friendly to me, and if I hadn't heard so many stories about his bad behavior in the break room, I'd have never known. The flirting was mild at first; the kind of attention that can be explained away by a gregarious personality. But then it became more aggressive.

I adjusted my uniform even more than I already did. I tried different bras to make my chest flatter. I wore less makeup. All I wanted was to do my work, get my paycheck, and go home.

Going to work became fraught with stress. When I felt his eyes on me, I couldn't ring up the groceries as quickly. I fumbled with counting change as he watched. We had requirements for scanning a certain number of items per minute, and I feared I'd lose my job if I didn't keep it together.

I was fast at ringing up groceries when he wasn't stressing me out, so I worked express checkout a lot. Many cashiers didn't like it because you had no down time, but it felt like a reprieve for me. It left little time for him to approach without customers intervening. But managers came to our registers often to enter override codes or bring us change, and he always found a way to touch me somehow. He ignored how it made me flinch each time.

He'd place a hand on my arm when speaking to me or run his hand across my back while talking to my customers. When I was in the cash office counting my till, he'd come up behind me and run his hands up and down my arms. He'd pull the schedule out and say things like, "If you're nice to me, I'll give you Friday off."

These were things that my ex-manager/ex-boyfriend did in an affectionate manner. But now, it was a man in his forties or fifties instead of a guy closer to my age. Unlike with my ex-boyfriend, I didn't welcome the attention at all. A knot formed in my stomach each time the man touched me, whereas with my ex-boyfriend, I'd felt nothing but butterflies.

But if this man was crossing a line, then it seemed like my ex had also, right? They were both adults, and I was a minor. The behavior was the same. The job title was the same. The only difference was that one was closer to my age, and I had welcomed his attention. I didn't know how to process that. Where *was* the line? Had I considered my ex-boyfriend's behavior okay only because I was attracted to him, and he was young? Was I doing something to bring on this attention? Was it my fault?

And then things got really confusing.

It was fairly easy to identify the women who played along with what the hiring manager wanted. His favoritism showed like a neon flashing sign. They spent half their shift in the cash office with him. They never had to work the express lane, the busiest job on the floor. In fact, they often didn't work the checkout lanes at all. They'd put labels on the shelves near the registers or take "go back" items to their respective shelves around the store. Coveted, easy tasks.

I realized then, even more than before, how similar the behavior between my two managers had been in many ways. My ex-boyfriend wasn't a predator, but he had definitely used his position to get in good with me. He let me know he would change the schedule if I asked. He let me work longer hours when I wanted and adjusted the time cards, since fifteen-year-olds could only work certain shifts. He served me beer when I came in to eat and after hours. I got to hang out with him in the office while others had to do hard, dirty jobs, like wash dishes or take out trash.

Don't get me wrong—I used him, too, although not always consciously. I loved the attention that came with having an older boyfriend and getting perks others didn't get. It was intoxicating. But I also liked him. And I assume the feeling was mutual.

As a teenager who was very naive about relationships and hugely insecure, I was confused about my different reactions to the same behaviors and what role I played in bringing them about. One thing I wasn't confused about then, though, was that the hiring manager behaved like a predator. And once I'd been at the job long enough for people to trust me more, I started to get more information than I ever wanted. I didn't know how to handle it. If adult women weren't doing anything, who was I to say something? I was the youngest, and it was only my second real job. I feared getting fired. I feared my parents' reaction even more.

Then, on break one day, a woman who was like a mama hen to me tearfully confessed that she regretted not speaking up. She said she had no choice. She needed a certain schedule for her kids. A couple other cashiers were in the room, and I asked why no one else had ever reported it to the main store manager. I'll never forget what one said next.

"I'd rather play his reindeer games every once in a while and get what I want than be miserable." Then she glared at me and told me to keep my mouth shut, because we'd have it worse if he left. So many years later, I wouldn't recognize her on the street if I saw her, but I'd probably recognize her voice. The phrase "reindeer games" is what cemented that snapshot in my memory. It was part of a line in a popular movie back then. I'd watched it enough that I had most of it memorized.

The woman had a daughter around my age. I wondered if she'd have reacted differently if her own daughter went to that job in my place.

The system functioned in its dysfunction. They hated the conditions; they hated him. But they didn't want anything to change. Some of them seemed to get what they wanted out of the relationship. Others seemed to feel they had no choice but to play along. Regardless, I received the message: don't make people uncomfortable, don't make waves, be polite.

The consequences of my questioning the system soon became clear. It was well known that I always obsessed about my till being accurate. Down to the penny. Never short even a nickel. I prided myself on it, and we had rules, of course. We couldn't be over or under by more than a certain amount, or we'd get written up. You had leeway if you gave someone an extra quarter once or punched in thirty-five cents on a coupon instead of twenty-five. But I'd never needed it before.

The day of the break room conversation, though? My till somehow came out two cents over the shortage limit. Enough to be written up. I counted it multiple times, but got the same result.

The next day, it happened again. Another amount that couldn't be chalked up to accident. Another shortage I hadn't caused. You only got three strikes with your till, and you were out. I had two. I didn't know what else to do but keep quiet and do my job.

My next shift after the two write-ups was on a day the hiring manager was off. Relief flowed through me when I picked up my till and didn't have to dodge his hands, but I traded one uncomfortable situation for another. I got the cold shoulder from a couple cashiers. It hurt. They'd always been nice to me; they didn't just decide one day to stop for no reason. It had to be because of the conversation in the break room.

I didn't know my last day at the grocery store would be my

last, but I should have. After I clocked in that day, the hiring manager handed me my till. He purposefully brushed against my breast. I sidestepped him and took my till to the counter. While I counted, he talked. Benign stuff at first, I thought, until I really started paying attention. He complimented my work and played up all the potential benefits of working at the store through high school and even college.

Then it took a disturbing turn.

He reminded me that he made the recommendations for raises, moves within the store, and transfers to other stores. He came up behind me, close enough that I felt his body heat. Without touching me otherwise, he leaned in and whispered in my ear. What he said isn't as important as how he made me feel in that moment: ashamed, tainted, dirty. Like I'd done something to bring on the unwanted attention.

His breath was hot on my neck as he spoke. I wanted to shrink away from it, but I had nowhere to go. Thankfully, he took a deep breath in and backed away.

I guess he expected me to turn around. To give him what he felt entitled to.

I so desperately wanted to confront him. To tell him off and throw my till at him, storming out with expletives and a rant to the main store manager. Instead, I said nothing and walked out the door to my assigned register. I prided myself on doing a good job, being a good employee, being a good girl. I was too scared of the consequences. So, I put my head down and got to work.

After my break, the hiring manager told me my till was short. It was an excessive amount. Obvious in how deliberate it was. A message to me that he was in control and could do whatever the hell he wanted. He didn't even wait until the end of my shift to do it; he fired me right then and there.

★ ★ ★

Other men and other incidents followed. Harassment, assault. Things I keep locked up deep in my brain for my own mental health. Things I have told very few people about, if any.

I thought it would get better as I got older, but working in restaurants and bars brought out some of the worst of it, to the point where I grew to expect the behavior and almost became numb to it. However, working in an office—even at a high level—hasn't protected me from being harassed, either. It's the same behavior, just wrapped in a more professional package.

For a large part of my life, my breasts continued to feel like weapons I was forced to carry. Loaded guns that could be used for good but usually resulted in harm. It was in the way men stared at them instead of looking at my face when I spoke. In the way clothes were designed to put them under a spotlight. In the words my male friends used, pushing me to "show off those assets" when I went on dates, as if the only thing I had to offer was mounds of flesh and fatty tissue.

So, I often hid my body in baggy, shapeless clothes. I used humor like a shield to hide my discomfort. I bit my tongue every time a man made an inappropriate remark or commented on my appearance. I brushed things off and stayed silent in situations when I shouldn't have. I didn't make waves. I was polite. I shrank myself down, when I should have been embracing who I was. I should have been using my voice and standing up to harassment. That came later, after many bad experiences in high school and college. After some hard lessons in law school and the professional world.

Eventually, I reported someone.

The first time was at my office job in college. A male

coworker walked into the women's bathroom where I was changing after work and took a long time to leave. My male boss dismissed it as a mistake and told me to let it go. He gave me a line I'd heard from men before: it's not a big deal.

After Human Resources stepped in, he changed his tune from "be polite" to reluctantly supporting me.

The second time had a different outcome. I ran a lottery pool for a group of attorneys working on a project. When I went to collect the money one week, a man waved his dollar bills in front of his crotch like a matador waving a red cape at a bull. It would have been demeaning enough if we'd been alone, but several other male attorneys stood nearby. They all laughed, even as he registered the horrified look on my face and shame colored his. All the years I'd spent in school to be a lawyer—all my hard work—faded away. I felt like I was back on that playground getting my bra snapped again. Like I'd done something wrong, just because I was a girl.

When I reported him, my supervisor backed me, and Human Resources agreed. The fact that they took me seriously and immediately acted wasn't what I'd expected after my previous experience. They asked me if I wanted him fired. I declined. I didn't want to take his job away; I just didn't want to work next to him every day. Truth be told, having them validate the severity of what had happened was enough.

He moved to another floor and gave me an apology and a gift. It was awkward, but I felt like he had genuinely apologized for his behavior. Later, the whole office moved to the same floor, and I had to pass him in the hall constantly until I left the company. All I could do at the time was shrug and say, *"C'est la vie."* That's life. But I did so knowing every day that I'd stood up for myself. That I'd chosen myself over being polite and dismissing behavior that made me uncomfortable.

One of my favorite podcasts is about true crime, and they often discuss how female victims sometimes get into bad situations because they were taught to be polite, even to strangers. The hosts' response to this?

"Fuck politeness."

Politeness is the enemy of the female of the species in so many ways, because the potential to encounter sexual harassment starts even before we put on that first bra. And no matter how much progress is made, there will always be people who harass others, sexually or otherwise. Every year I have at least one personal experience that reminds me of that. But you don't have to stay quiet and internalize your discomfort.

You don't have to view your body as a loaded weapon, like I did.

You don't have to silence your voice, like I did.

Call out harassers. Speak for those who are too afraid, and let others speak for you when you can't. There can be consequences for harassers and predators of all types—and there should be.

You were given a voice for a reason. Use it.

Fuck politeness.

★ ★ ★ ★ ★

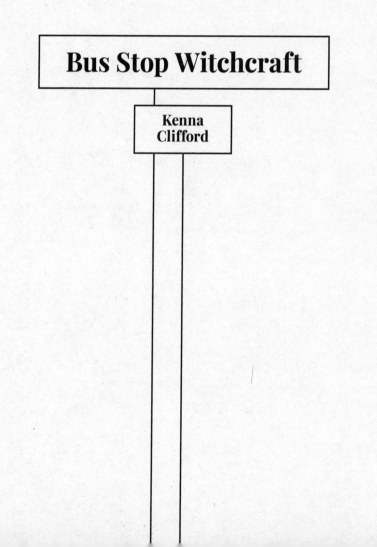

Bus Stop Witchcraft

**Kenna
Clifford**

About a week before I left for college, I went out for coffee with one of my close friends from home. I had a few days left free from packing for my new life as a film student in Vancouver, and we both knew it would be the last time we would see each other before December. Until then, I would be living in a city completely different from the small town we both grew up in. Between bad inside jokes and goodbyes, the part I remember most vividly is the advice he left me with—though perhaps it's more fitting to call it a comprehensive list of ways to avoid creepy dudes at parties. It was framed as a joke, something meant to make me laugh, despite my anxiety. But the twinge of concern in his voice made it clear that he understood there was some truth in what he was saying.

There are rules to living in a world where our bodies are

framed as things to consume. We learn them quickly. They are rooted in our brains from the time we learn how to walk and talk and look enough like girls to make us targets. By the time I was thirteen, I had already learned to instinctively cover any inch of skin that would invite prying eyes. Everyone knows that if you leave a drink alone, it's not yours anymore. When you walk down the street at night, you shouldn't make eye contact with people passing by. A smile might be a nicety to you, but to someone else, it might be an invitation.

Like family recipes, little whispers of wisdom like these trickle from person to person, each a home-brewed recipe for fear. I was once told by a friend of my grandmother to hide a twenty-dollar bill in my bra in case I needed a means to get home safely. "You should go to Krav Maga classes," my mom suggested before I moved out. And for even the seemingly simple task of walking at night, we are bombarded with news articles and ads on how to survive. Martial arts training and modest clothing definitely shouldn't be requirements on my checklist for transit safety.

After saying goodbye to both my town and the security blanket of familiarity, I became acutely aware of how incredibly alone I would be in the city. Taking public transit was new to me, and the fear of what could happen to me on a bus at night spiked my anxiety to the point of physical discomfort. I would carefully strategize my seat, knowing that sitting in the wrong place on the way back to school might open up an opportunity for wandering hands. I would curl into myself, so as to take up as little space as possible. After all, it's easier to feel safe when you are small enough not to be noticed.

The world is a lot colder when you constantly have to think about your safety over making connections. When you have to think about the steps of getting to and from where you're going without being harassed. Even in areas that are considered home, I still had to deal with vulgar things spit through car windows at my friends and me, or echoing behind us as we walked down the street. While swimming at the riverside, two boys walking past said that wearing a bikini was "asking them" to say sexually violating things to us. Even though I was living in a town that was objectively considered safe, somewhere I had grown up, I felt comfortable out at night only when I had someone at my side who understood what I really meant when I said I was afraid of the dark. We put up a brave face and stuck our middle fingers proudly in the air as if it didn't hurt us. It's not easy being told to your face how worthless someone thinks you are.

With the rise of the #MeToo movement, it's easier to speak more openly about the complications that come with existing as female presenting in the twenty-first century. And yet, when I was asked to contribute to an anthology addressing the #MeToo movement, I was immediately conflicted. There is a kind of cultural awareness now, a general platform to hear the voices of the harassed, but that cultural awareness often represents a small population of privileged women. My first thought was that, as a seventeen-year-old white girl raised in a mostly upper-middle-class town, I would be taking away from the strength of voices that really mattered. I worried that my experiences would not be considered important enough.

I am incredibly lucky to be growing up in a world on the forefront of change. The bravery of people with lungs full of passion and voices that are finally being heard has opened new opportunities for my generation. There is a shift in the way we see the world, no longer accepting actions that have been tolerated for years without consequences. We still have a long way to go, of course. But I feel the current pushing toward change. Along with others, I have the privilege to experience the full force of this movement, and I am so incredibly lucky to feel the effects of empowerment flow into my own generation. And if there is anything I have learned from growing up at this pivotal point in history, it's that every single person has a story to share—including me.

I'm aware I've been born into a position of power not afforded to all, and I am incredibly grateful to have this opportunity both to speak and be heard. Nevertheless, I want to stress that my experience is not the only experience, and it is so incredibly important to raise up the stories of people who have been silenced, no matter what they look like or where they come from. I think it's easier for a lot of people to stomach the idea that sexual harassment is something that happens only to a select few, a certain demographic of specific women who have the platform to speak about it. However, there is room for all stories in this movement, from all experiences and walks of life. It is our job to support them. Refuse to talk over them. Strengthen the voices and legs of our brothers, sisters, and everyone in between with unconditional love and support. We are a coven bound by whispers and incantations, sacred rituals and protection spells. There is only one requirement to join our renegade—the choice to give respect.

When the #MeToo allegations first came to light, it was easy to assume that the dark underbelly of sexual harassment and assault applied only to the entertainment industry. There's a beautiful veil placed over filmmaking; one made of golden statues and red carpets and fancy dresses. We idolize artists like we once did during the Renaissance, as if they have some sort of auratic, godly quality that places them above us. It wasn't until I found my passion for making films myself that I began to fully understand that real human people made films. Maybe it sounds absurd. I mean, I *knew* that people made movies. But to some extent, it was easier to imagine the film industry as some kind of smoke-and-mirror illusion that willed characters into existence. The public doesn't see what happens between takes and closed curtains. It's easy to hide things when you have access to editing equipment. I think that's why it took so long to uncover the despicable acts perpetrated by artists in powerful positions. It's all too easy to turn a blind eye to the bad behaviors of people who make good art, because on a core level, it feels like trying to empathize with an illusion. I have had conversations with people who insist on defending directors who have not only been accused, but found guilty of acts of sexual harassment and assault. Of course, it's never a statement that these people are good, but rather that they are entitled to a bubble of protection because of their contributions. They are still seen as something above us, and thus their actions are an afterthought. They are no longer held down by the weight of compassion. Like ghosts, they float through consciousness without the tethers of humanity. This glorification of innovators has allowed despicable people to feel sheltered from the consequences of their actions for far too long. Even now, it still feels like they sit on a pedestal the size of Mount Olympus.

The truth is that they are people. *We* are people. And sexual assault is not something that is restricted to above the clouds.

At only eighteen, I have heard too many stories from people I know well, people I care about. Sexual harassment isn't contained to a small group; it happens on the same street as you, the same school, the same party, even in the same room. It thrives in little places between couch cushions and broken boundaries. It is not a gendered issue, though it is born in the belly of misogyny, a beast that has been rooted in Western society and watered by an intoxicating mixture of media and culture long before we knew the words to describe it. It does not just affect white women. It does not just affect straight women. It does not just affect cis women. It does not just affect women.

During my first year of high school, I realized that gay women are considered inherently erotic. It's not noticeable at first, the idea that queer relationships exist—for some people—purely for the pleasure of erotic gaze. It didn't really settle into the forefront of my mind until I walked down the street with my friend and her girlfriend holding hands. I heard them getting catcalled from the side of the road by strangers who seemed to believe that their romance was public property. I still watch my friends stand away from each other, hiding any sign of closeness to avoid unwanted attention. It's discouraging, to say the least, especially whilst navigating your own sexuality.

It's a scary idea that being attracted to women has to mean vulgarity, so full of prying eyes and opinions. My current partner had expressed how scared he was when he first wanted to kiss me. I used to playfully tease him for the way he would put his face close to me but never quite initiate anything. He told me he was scared of confusing signals or putting me in a situation where I did not feel safe. In a way, realizing I was bisexual felt just like that. Deep down, it felt like I would never be able to kiss a girl or look at someone romantically without feeling predatory. We are so used to being told relationships are about pursuit, and I was scared that being allowed into the spaces considered havens by straight girls would make me a Trojan horse. Like the sexualization of female relationships would somehow be the outside understanding of my inner feelings, and not the intricacies of platonic and romantic relationships. It felt like I couldn't be friends with a girl without seeming like my actions would be misinterpreted. I had been to sleepovers, shared beds with my female friends. I didn't want the recognition of my bisexuality to mean that those things were anything other than acts of friendship. So I stayed quiet about my feelings. I would hide inside the stalls in changing rooms in case someone caught any glimpse of quiet curiosity, real or imagined, in my eyes. I didn't come out until about two years after labeling my identity. I am often still very selective in who I tell about my romantic preferences. I suppose with the admittance of this in a book, it's not particularly secret anymore. I deliberated long and hard about whether or not I wanted to include this, knowing that so many would read it.

But honestly? I am finally okay with that. Gay women are constantly told that their love is purely sexual, a show put on for the eyes of others. Try to claim this kind of love as something for yourself, and it's no longer acceptable. Maybe my choice to let this be known will help someone else feel okay with appreciating the freckles on the girl across the room, or quietly noticing the way someone's hair falls down their back. Queerness is constantly fetishized by television and film despite being demeaned by the people who write the characters. We are regarded as a visual aid for projective fantasies. And no matter who I love, no matter their gender, there will always be an undercurrent of doubt that lurks below the surface. A kind of doubt that isn't from any insecurity about my own sexual identification, but rather the collateral of the acceptance of that part of me. I know that taking the label also means I'll never fully fit into any space without feeling like an attraction. But being able to proudly wear my identity is a small step toward attaching a brain and a personality and a voice to the body I have. If you are in the same place as I once was, I hope you know that you are not wrong to feel this way.

You are not predatory. Your love does not belong to the eyes of others. And kissing girls who care about you is pretty great.

To me, the #MeToo movement means choosing to take back sovereignty of our bodies in a world where it is radical to feel comfortable. It is the act of saying, "We are more than something to look at." No matter how many times you have been belittled or silenced, if you have the courage to keep going, you can create change. I have seen it with my own eyes. The existence of this book proves it.

I find it ironic that one of the major criticisms of the tidal wave of assault allegations is that it is becoming a "witch hunt." As if the words we speak are fantasy. As if the people who call us witch hunters do not come from the same people who burned our ancestors at the stake for wanting more than a subservient life. Those women were victims, every bit as much as so many people today. And in their honor, I choose to wear a pointed hat with pride, especially if it means I get to share even an ounce of the magic and power that they could conjure. Because I'm tired of curling up on buses and pretending to be small. I am tired of mapping out escape routes in my head. I am tired of living in fear.

So, consider this essay our formal initiation ritual into a coven of love and acceptance. If you have ever been silenced, know that this is your time to speak. Woven within you are the spells of a million scorned who know now what reckoning tastes like. Stand with them, gain power from their stories. Take the fear that has been forced into your throat and use it to fuel the storm of truth. And finally, don't ever let anyone steal your tongue from your mouth.

You have teeth for a reason.

★ ★ ★ ★ ★

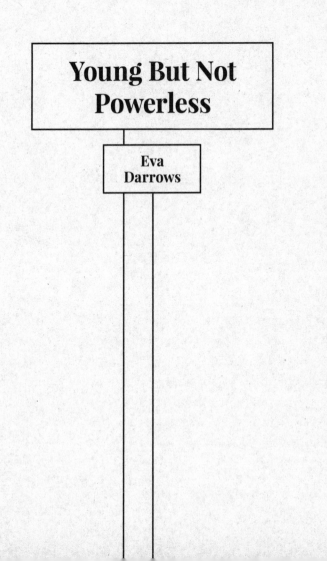

Young But Not Powerless

Eva Darrows

The term *broken stair* (or in some circles, *missing stair*) didn't exist when I was a teenager. It wasn't penned until 2012, by blogger Cliff Pervocracy. In case you, reader, don't know what it means, it's a turn of phrase used to describe a serial harasser—usually a *cis man—who's never been *officially* outed or reported, but his victims have whispered about him in an effort to keep other people safe.

"Oh, _____? He's handsy."

"Don't be alone with _____. He's bad news."

"_____ is here. Be careful."

The broken stair is the person you avoid because you don't feel safe reporting their behavior in order to "fix them"—much like the broken stair in the actual stairwell is the step you avoid instead of fixing it with a hammer and nail.

Make sense?

I had a teacher who was a notorious broken stair. I had a couple, actually, but let's start with Mr. Mathers (not his real name), the woodshop teacher. The upperclassmen warned the lowerclassmen about him, who in turn warned the new lowerclassmen when they eventually became upperclassmen. It was the Circle of Life, harassment-style, and it was, in retrospect, terrible. In our defense, we didn't have the discourse then that we have now. We knew what rape was, of course. We knew sexual harassment was a thing, but mostly as it related to politicians being scummy (not much has changed in twenty-something years, I guess). It wasn't something we realized actually applied *to us*, as high school students. It was "bigger" than us, at fourteen years old—an adult problem. So when we were told Mr. Mathers, a teacher in his fifties, was a creep, we did what everyone before us had done: we did our best to avoid him, and we made sure other girls knew about his tendencies.

Mr. Mathers liked the chesty girls, you see.

You didn't wear anything remotely low cut with him around.

You'd think it'd be a simple enough thing to do—to report to the principal or the dean or really anyone over Mr. Mathers's head that he made a lot of girls uncomfortable with his ogling. People recoil at the notion of pedophilia, after all, but numerous things made this complicated. For one, he didn't do anything so explicit that they'd arrest him. He wasn't grabbing girls in their chest area or propositioning them for sex in his car. He was a much more subtle bag of gross. He was a woodshop teacher, so he stood over or behind the girls and pressed against them while he taught them. He stared down our shirts while we worked the machinery—

shamelessly, even—almost every time. When he talked to us, he didn't look us in the face, but in the boobs.

Ick, right?

"But," fourteen-year-old me protests, "what are we going to do about it?" No one told us this was a reportable offense, or that we should report it, or even *how* to report it. Mr. Mathers was awful, but there were worse things he could have been doing, so it was easiest to just let the whisper network do its thing and wear turtlenecks for the rest of our natural lives.

(Not a healthy outlook by any stretch of the imagination, but we were young and did what girls have been trained to do since the beginning of time—accept the responsibility of harassment not by insisting our perpetrators stop being awful human beings, but by getting better at protecting ourselves from them.)

The second reason reporting seemed daunting was that the guy had been in the school system so long, his creepy behavior may have transcended an entire generation. He knew everyone in our small town, and a lot of his cis male students thought he hung the moon. Woodshop is way more interesting than, say, math to a lot of kids, so Mr. Mathers stood out as one of the "fun ones" and reaped the benefits of his popularity. To complicate matters further, his sister was a long-standing English teacher who I affectionately referred to as Cerberus. She was one of my favorite teachers, despite her claws and acid spit, so to go after Mr. Mathers was to go after a totally separate, much-loved teacher, albeit indirectly.

It's hard enough to stand up to a grown-up when he's thirty years your senior, but his befanged sister, too? Nope. Nah. Not happening. That's too much.

And so, Mr. Mathers got passes. For years and years, until his retirement, he got passes. Woodshop was a requirement in our school (opposite of home economics the other half of the year), so graduating class after graduating class endured weird staring and awkward bodily contact until he aged out of the system. Did we survive it? Sure, but it was uncomfortable, and in a place of learning—in any place, really, but particularly in a school—there should be no room for that kind of behavior.

Except there was room for Mr. Mathers.

And more, come to find out.

Mr. Forester (again, not his real name) came around the next year. He was another well-liked teacher who "could hang" with the kids and would often cross that boundary between educator and your buddy by just being *a little bit cooler* than the rest of the teachers. He taught American History and made it fun with lots of games and jokes. He kicked his trash can when he thought someone wasn't paying attention, so you always stayed on your toes for fear of a startle, but he made being involved with the lesson worthwhile by just... being himself. He was super charismatic.

This man was Mr. Mathers's age, if not a little older, and again, he'd been part of our high school for years. Another similarity Mr. Mathers and Mr. Forester shared, beyond their tenure? Mr. Forester's wife was also an English teacher, two classrooms down the hall. I'm not going to say that you shouldn't have familial relations working in the same school system, but I would like to point out that the behaviors outlined in both of my examples were complicated by admiration for Mr. Mathers's sister in example one, and Mr. Forester's wife in example two. Scared kids had to wrestle with not only the knowledge that they'd be implicating teachers who were super popular with the student body if they reported, but they'd also be impacting *other* teachers they held in high esteem.

While there are zero circumstances under which Mr. Mathers's behaviors were tolerable, I could (and would) argue that Mr. Forester was the worse predator. He didn't target swaths of kids, but singled out one, and that one happened to be one of my best friends. For the purposes of this essay, I'll call her Suzanne. Suzanne was a pretty girl, and popular. She was smart, athletic, really had the whole package together, but there was a vulnerability about her, too, and it made her a perfect target for Mr. Forester.

See, Suzanne had been involved with horses all her life and took riding lessons from a woman named Jeanne, who'd pretty much adopted her as family. Jeanne died unexpectedly the year Suzanne had Mr. Forester as her teacher. Suzanne was a little lost, a lot sad, and looking for comfort. Mr. Forester was willing to provide it—and proceeded to provide it inappropriately *for two years*.

I called Suzanne while I was writing this, to ensure I'd get the details of her victimization correct. Over the phone, she outlined an extended block of time where she was groomed— and she recognizes that behavior now as grooming—to allow Mr. Forester to get close. At first it was after-school hangouts. I sometimes accompanied Suzanne to these, particularly in the beginning, catching glimpses of what compelled her to keep visiting him during her free time. Let me state again: Mr. Forester was the "cool" teacher, and he wasn't making time every day for other students—just her and, by proxy, me. Being one of the two girls in his classes mature enough to warrant loose, hang-out talk with the cool guy felt nice.

And for a girl in Suzanne's situation, who didn't have the best relationship with her father, and who was looking for an adult friend to fill the gap Jeanne left behind? It felt necessary, and so things progressed.

Casual touches eventually turned to him giving her shoulder rubs. What made this so insidious was it developed over months to years—it probably took six months for him to start touching her at all, and once he started, the touches escalated, again, slowly. Hugs. Short ones. Then longer ones. All in his classroom with the door closed. Eventually, he asked to kiss her on the cheek. She agreed. After that, she noticed that he'd take out a roll of wintergreen Lifesavers whenever she walked in the room after school.

He was expecting more kisses, you see, and if shoulder rubs had become hugs, and hugs had become cheek kisses...well?

You can see where this was going.

At some point during Suzanne's grooming, stories began to get back to her about Mr. Forester having an unfortunate and weird relationship with some of the players on the basketball team he used to coach. It's that broken stair thing all over again; he had a bad reputation, and the girls passed that knowledge down from class to class. While Suzanne didn't immediately jump to the conclusion that she'd become "that girl"—in fact, by her own admission, she felt loyalty to her friend, and wanted to protect Mr. Forester from any accusations—as he pushed the physical intimacies further, she eventually figured out that she was part of a disastrous cycle.

She stopped going to see him when the kiss requests/demands got to be too much. Weirdly, a few months after she *stopped* visiting, she was pulled into an impromptu meeting with her parents and the superintendent to discuss her relationship with Mr. Forester. It seems someone had witnessed something at the end of the previous school year between the two of them and reported it. Not too long after that, Mr.

Forester had a heart attack and left the school for health reasons, so there's no real resolution to what could or would have happened with him with future classes. However, it is at least somewhat reassuring to know that another teacher had clued in that Suzanne was being victimized.

When looking back at my years (and years and years) of history with harassment, I decided not to focus on my everyday interactions with boys my own age, but rather on what I see as the most egregious examples of attackers preying on more vulnerable people. Both men in my stories held positions of power. They had respect among not only the student body, but their peers, too. And both violated the trust teens had given them for personal gain. In the case of Mr. Mathers, he was clearly getting a sexual thrill at the expense of girls thirty to forty years his junior. In the case of Mr. Forester, he was... I don't even know what. It's not good in any scenario, and gives me *Lolita* vibes that make my skin crawl.

It goes without saying that not all cool, friendly, or popular teachers are predators. It also goes without saying that some are, and they will use the tools at their disposal to hurt teens. The onus of sexual harassment and sex assault should never be on the victims to act less like victims. It should always, always be on the attackers to stop victimizing people. That said, understanding that there are people who will prey upon you, particularly if they lord authority over you, can be pivotal to our survival. Keep your eyes open. Protect your bodily autonomy as best you can. And most importantly?

Report if you can.

That's not as simple as I make it sound, I know. It's hard, it's daunting, it's usually a messy process that rarely respects the dignity of the victims, but if you are in a position to talk about your harassment, tell a parent. A guardian. A therapist.

Someone you trust in the faculty. There *are* good teachers out there, I promise; heaven knows they didn't get involved in teaching for the money. Talk to them, and ask them for their help if you're able.

And if you're not, I understand that, too, and a hug from me to you. None of this is easy. I look forward to the day we stop saying "Me Too," and start saying "Never again."

★ ★ ★ ★ ★

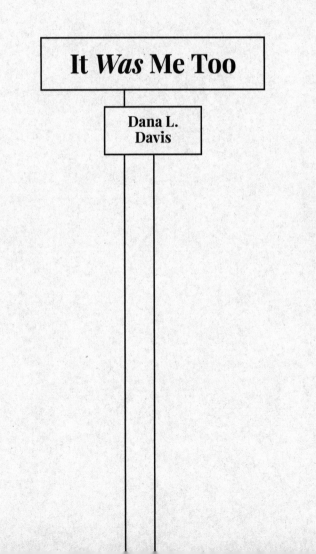

It *Was* Me Too

Dana L.
Davis

I used to walk past a giant cornfield to get to school in the mornings. Sometimes my older brother and I might even yank corn from the stalks and bring it home to roast. The big event each year in my town was the county fair, and every day, when the final school bell rang, I'd catch the city bus to my after-school job—packing deli meat at a meat factory. That was small-town living.

But I journeyed far away from my hometown in the heart of the Midwest to seek out my life's purpose. Red-carpet events became my new normal. Warner Brothers, NBC, and CBS became my new backyard. Yet while most would find the life-style of an actress in Hollywood to be pretty exciting, life for me was far from a dream. I was working my dream job, sure, but far from *enjoying* the lifestyle I'd earned. One day, though, I would take a brave step toward making that change...

I was searching frantically for my keys one Tuesday morning while a *Headline News* story about a capsized fishing boat blared through my television speakers. If I didn't get out the door and into my car in the next five minutes, I was sure to be caught in rush-hour traffic and late to an important audition. Auditions always made me a bit anxious, so the thought of being late had me literally running in and out of every room in my Hollywood condo looking for my lost keys. I opened cupboards in the dining room, drawers in my bedroom, and even checked inside the freezer (because I'd left them in there once) before I noticed my keys peeking out from under the couch. *How'd they get under there?* Just as I rushed into the living room and dropped to the floor to retrieve them, my cell phone vibrated in my hand. I pressed the button to accept the call.

"Hi, Dana. You got a second?"

It was my agent. And though I was in a desperate rush to get on the 405 Freeway, something in the tone of her voice made me sit on the edge of the couch cushion and click off the TV instead.

"Everything okay?"

I must've sounded as worried as I felt, because she laughed and said, "Everything's fine! But I do need to sort of...talk to you about something."

I took a nervous breath. "Sure. Yeah." I gripped my keys and rested my forearms on my knees. I felt nauseated. Something was off. Something was wrong.

"I just hung up with Jeremy Pineski," she explained.

I swallowed hard. Jeremy was the producer of a series I was working on. Why had he called my agent?

"Am I fired?" I asked softly.

"What? No. Nothing like that at all!" she assured me, though I couldn't help but notice her troubled tone. "He just seemed really sad."

"Sad?" I asked, confused. Jeremy was one of the nicest guys I'd ever worked with. Quirky. Silly. With stylish square glasses, signature scruff, and a contagious laugh. The sort of new-ager who gushed about Spider-Man remakes instead of politics and stood in long lines at comic-cons to get pictures with his favorite superheroes. He was the very antithesis of sad.

"He thinks you're unhappy on the show."

"Wait. *What?* Why on Earth would he think that? I love the show."

"He says it's your vibe. Like, when you guys wrap for the day, he says you're always the first to leave. You almost run out of the studio. You seem a bit closed off. Unapproachable."

Was that really how I came off? When I was working on a show I loved? With a producer I admired? "I'm sorry, Kristin," I started. "But I'm socially awkward. I race out of there because I don't know what to say to them."

"Stop it. You're not awkward! It's just..." She paused, seemingly gathering her thoughts. "There's an element to this business that you're not fully grasping. It's more than the work. You have to check in. You *have* to be social."

"Why? The work I do is good. I'm doing a good job for them. Right?"

"Right. They love you. But next time, maybe stay for a bit after? Lighten up. Laugh."

There was a tense moment of silence between us before I said, "Can you please tell them I'm happy and I love the show?"

"I can tell them. Sure," my agent replied. "But why don't you? Next time you see them. Say just that."

We said our goodbyes, and I glanced at the clock perched

above my fireplace. I was definitely going to be late to my audition. The fear of having to chat with producers at work had left me shaken; with sweaty palms and a racing heart. Keeping a comfortable distance had always been my thing. My suit of armor. And now, with a simple phone call, my agent was asking me to change it up. Let down my guard. Allow my light to shine. I knew in order to do that, I had to check back in with the girl I left home in the Midwest—the one with ears of corn sticking out of her backpack on the way home from school.

The girl I had worked hard to leave behind.

I was only a kid in elementary school when I was sexually assaulted. I remember the day vividly, almost as if it's a movie that's stored in my mind. All I have to do is push a button to relive it in vivid HD technicolor. I dare not ever push it, though at times it can play on its own, and I become a prisoner to the unwanted memories. Victimized once again.

The day I was assaulted started out as a special day. For some reason my mom bought me a new outfit. It was purple, my favorite color at the time, and she tied purple ribbons in my hair, made of soft, braided yarn.

I looked so pretty as I danced in front of the mirror and smiled at my reflection.

I was a real princess walking to school that morning. No tiara, but that didn't stop me from imagining myself waving the royal wave I'd seen on TV as I moved into the yard of Madison Elementary. I held my head a bit higher for sure. It was like everyone else could see it was a special day for me, too. Was it the ribbons tied so delicately around my ponytails? The new outfit? Maybe I would ask my mom to make me look this pretty all the time.

I was shining so bright. I was on top of the world. Or at least on top of the small town I grew up in.

At lunch I noticed two boys desperate to get my attention. Smiling at *me?* No boy ever really noticed me before. It was the ribbons, I thought. I reached up to make sure they were still secure and in place, and the boys' smiles stretched across their faces. They waved. I blushed and waved back, then stared down at my tray of cafeteria food. Another girl leaned over and whispered in my ear.

"I think they like you."

Me? How exciting. I couldn't believe it.

After lunch was recess, and I was the purple princess of the playground when I once again noticed the two boys staring at me from a distance. But now there were more—about five of them in total. All focused on *me!* This truly was my day. My moment to shine.

The boys started rushing toward me. Did they want to talk to me? Tell me how much they liked me now? Oh, I know! I grinned. We were going to play tag! I loved tag!

I took off running, moving fast around the playground with the boys close behind. I ran and ran, laughing as the sun kissed my skin. My ponytails bouncing on my shoulders as I raced excitedly.

Suddenly they were close. Running so close behind me. Too close.

My freedom now seemed reckless. None of my friends were close by. I was alone, unsure what my next move should be. What would happen if they caught me? I tried to look around for aides on the playground, but I didn't see any nearby. And it was too late, anyway, because I was caught.

The boys formed a tight circle around me. One grabbed my arms and pinned them behind my back.

I screamed.

But another placed a hand over my mouth.

I couldn't move.

I couldn't yell for help.

I couldn't see through my tears.

And then it happened. Right on the playground of my elementary school, hands reached down my pants and fingers entered me. Robbing me of an innocent youth.

There was nothing I could physically do to fight them off. I could only wait until they'd finished whatever game they thought they were playing. When it was finally over, the boys laughed and dispersed, leaving me a shattered and broken version of my former self.

After a few moments, I managed to get my bearings and ran to find a playground aide. I pointed toward the boys, who had all scattered in different directions, returned to their normal playground activities, as if a very grave injustice had not just taken place.

"Them!" I screamed. "They hurt me."

"Who?" the concerned aide replied.

I was able to identify them all.

"What did they do?"

But I could only wail in agony.

The aide quickly rushed me to the office. I sat on a cold metal chair for what seemed like hours (though I'm sure it was only a couple of minutes) until at last, all the boys were ushered into the office, as well. No longer laughing and sneering, they took their seats across from me, their smiles replaced with expressions I couldn't identify at the time.

I wiped my nose with the back of my hand. I would tell on them. They would all be punished—every last one of them would pay for what they'd done to me.

When the principal came out to speak with us, she addressed me first. "What happened, Dana?"

She handed me a tissue as I continued to wail inconsolably. Eventually, I looked over at my attackers. And suddenly, I *could* read the looks on their faces.

It was embarrassment. It was complete and utter humiliation. I must've worn a similar expression myself.

Later in life, I would learn a better word for what rushed over me in that moment—shame.

"Dana," the principal repeated. "Please tell me what happened?"

Could I admit to the principal what had happened? It was my fault, after all. My stupid ribbons. My new purple clothes. My happy smile. My glow. I'd shined too bright that day. That's why they chose me.

"They…threw rocks at me," I sobbed. "That's all."

The principal nodded and patted me on the back as if it was no big deal. As if rocks being thrown on the playground was nothing to be so upset about. She sent me back to class, and I took my very first walk of shame. I was only seven years old, but I suspected that everyone in the hallway could sense it as I moved by.

They knew. Dear God, they *knew*.

I hung my head low and wiped my tears.

I never told a living soul about my assault on the playground in elementary school, convinced it was my fault, confident that if I hadn't shined so bright that day, the boys would never have noticed me. As time passed, that shame settled deep into the core of who I was, where it festered and fermented until it turned into something much darker. Depression. Self-hate. I became determined to make sure I was never hurt in that way again.

So I adopted a new mantra: *Keep your distance. Lower your head. Dim your light.*

Years later, at a new school and living in a new neighborhood, I happened upon one of the boys who had assaulted me. He was walking down the street. Somehow, I mustered the courage to approach him. I tapped him on the shoulder, and he stopped and turned around to face me.

"You hurt me," I said.

I was shaking. He was, too. He remembered. The shame was still there for him. I could see it clearly when he lowered his head to avoid my eyes.

"I-it wasn't me," he stammered. "I d-didn't do it. It was the other boys. They were bad. It was them."

"But you were there!" I cried. "You were there!"

For he was the boy who held back my arms. He was certainly one of the guilty.

"I'm sorry," he whispered. And then he ran away. Down the street. Leaving me alone on my walk home from school.

After hanging up with my agent, I missed my audition and spent the day home alone. I needed time to prepare. Not just for the next day at work with my producers, but for *all* the days to come. How long could I continue to live this way? How long was I going to hide? I knew it was time to reconnect with that little girl who was hurt so long ago.

I started by taking my agent's advice. When we finished recording the next episode of the season, I went into the area where all the producers were mingling. There was no longer a thick pane of glass separating us. No microphones and sheets of script paper strewn about on stands. Only a bit of empty space between us now. I could reach out and touch them if I wanted. They could reach out and touch me, too.

My palms were sweaty as I mumbled out a barely audible, "How are you guys?"

They looked genuinely shocked I was speaking. But they were kind. Receptive.

The exchange lasted only about sixty seconds. Before I left, I walked over to the executive producer and head writer.

"Hi, Jeremy." I smiled brightly to cover my all-encompassing fear.

"Dana Davis!" he exclaimed with the Hollywood swagger I had grown to admire; so cool and confident, so full of life. So free. He snatched off his square-rimmed glasses and leaned back in his chair, running a hand over his signature scruff. "You were amazing today."

"Thank you," I replied. "And hey... I love this show. I love you guys. I'm just...shy. I wanted you to know. Sorry I've been so... I dunno...weird?" I forced out an awkward laugh.

He set down his glasses and reached out his hand to shake mine. "Dana, we're just happy to have you. You're perfect for this character, and as long as you're happy, I'm happy. You sure you're happy?"

"I'm happy," I replied. "Promise."

It was a huge effort not to cry. I saved my tears for the car ride home as the shame engulfed me once again. Shame that turned icy cold in my heart. Like a lifetime plague. Would it never leave? Would it always rise up like bile in my throat?

When I began to hear of women in my industry confessing their stories of assault at the hands of industry men, I felt numb. Friends began to call. *Dana, did you hear about this one? Dana, did you hear about that one? Has it happened to you too?*

"No," I would always declare. *"Not me too."*

I was only a child when I'd decided men could not be

trusted. And I'd done a good job of keeping myself protected—or at least I thought I had.

"*Dana,*" my agents would say. "*A director wants to have a work
session with you at his house.*"

"*Oh, really?*" I'd reply, heart racing. "*I can't make it that day.
Maybe we can just chat on the phone?*"

"*Dana!*" A producer would smile at me. "*Come to my office!
I want to show you some of the scenes we shot yesterday.*"

"*Is that right?*" I'd swallow. "*I'll be there in a few!*"

Of course, I'd never show.

"*Hey, Dana!*" a coworker would call out. "*We're all headed
out for drinks. Interested?*"

"*Definitely!*" I'd reply excitedly. But I'd make sure not to
answer my phone.

I wasn't really protecting myself. I was running. I remained
as frozen as I was that day in the principal's office. Still shoul-
dering blame after so many years. Allowing the lifestyle I had
earned to pass me by. Somehow, those women coming forward, sharing their stories of sexual assault, made me realize
that I was *tired* of running. It was time to confess to my reality. To finally say that it *was* me too.

It is.

I was once a little girl who never had the courage to tell
what should have been told. Instead, I chose to shoulder the
blame, to dim my light and hide. So today, I take another
step toward healing by sharing my story, and admitting that
it *is* me too. It's my hope that the little girl in women of all
ages will have the courage to tell their stories, as well, take
the necessary steps to heal, and claim the right to shine bright
once again.

★ ★ ★ ★ ★

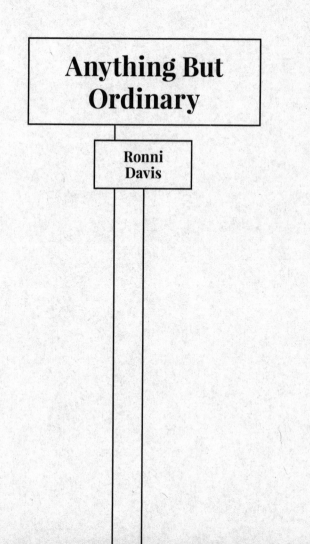

Anything But Ordinary

Ronni Davis

I never told anyone my story. And yet, the hardest part of writing this essay wasn't deciding whether or not I should tell—it was deciding which story to tell. Like too many of us, I had a lot to choose from.

I attended high school in inner-city Cleveland, Ohio. I hated it. I knew it wasn't going to be like the schools on TV or in movies, but when I found myself on the verge of tears during lunch on my very first day, I knew it was going to be a long four years.

I felt so alone, even though I was in a sea of people. I didn't have anything in common with them. My interests were on the opposite side of the spectrum. I wrote stories and stories and stories. I dreamed of being famous. I wanted to be extraordinary!

The people around me seemed to live in the "now," mainly worrying about the latest music videos or urban fashion. I instinctively knew that the stuff I liked would get made fun of, so I kept quiet, absorbing the cacophony around me. The bravado, the outdoing each other. The "I don't give a fuck" attitude. Maybe it was a front. A way of trying to survive day-to-day in a world that constantly stacked the deck against them.

Against us. Me.

I often wondered where I fit in, born into a family of people with brown skin, and me being very light with golden hair and hazel eyes. I spent hours in front of the mirror, wishing I could be brown like everyone else in my family. But I'm "neutral beige," according to the pressed powder at Sephora. Number 200 Fenty foundation. White-passing skin...but ultimately, I was a *little black girl*, and with that came special rules. Don't act too "white" (even though most of my interests were "white" ones). Don't act too "fast" (and when you're a black girl, any move—rolling your shoulders, shaking your butt when you're dancing, snapping your fingers—is considered "fast"). Don't play too closely with boys. *Any* boys.

I was constantly in a battle between who I was and who everyone wanted me to be.

One year, when I was in high school, we kept journals in class. Mine was probably full of passages about how much I liked New Kids on the Block. That's pretty much all I wrote/talked/thought about back then. I must have also written some stuff regarding struggling with my identity, because eventually, some classmates got a hold of the journal, read it, and decided that I was the class Oreo. I don't know if the mean-ing still holds, but back then, people used the term "Oreo" to make fun of "black people who act white."

After reading my journal, and publicly discussing the con-tents, people started telling me I should "act my color."

Act my color. Because apparently, *I* was the one who did something wrong—not them, who had read my school assignments and judged me based on those words. *Act my color.* Like it was my fault they disliked me. *Act my color.* Like I told them to read my journal, even if they weren't going to like what they saw.

I don't remember feeling particularly angry, but I do re-member embarrassment. They'd invaded my privacy, and now they were using words they should have never seen against me. I think a prouder girl would have stood up to them, but I convinced myself that I deserved their scorn. *I shouldn't have written it. I should have stopped them from reading it. I should have made smarter choices!*

I should have "acted my color."

Except in my mind, "acting a color" wasn't a Thing, and I was just being ME. Even though I was still trying to figure out exactly who I was.

This is what I did know: I hated living in the inner city, where angry men shot guns outside my bedroom window. I was jealous of my best friend, who, on marathon phone calls, would describe her glamorous day-to-day life in private school, with sports teams and after-school activities and cute white boys and friends who drove expensive cars and whose parents had vacation homes and country club memberships. She was a black girl who'd pulled herself out of inner-city high school life. I hated that I didn't do that, too.

I hated that no one, besides her, seemed to believe I could

ever do it. And I hated that people made me feel guilty about *wanting* to do it. But nothing stopped me from wanting that ideal life. That "white" life. And I just knew I was bad for feeling and thinking the way I did.

For being me.

Because maybe I *was* an "Oreo."

And not being proud of who I was? That deserved punishment.

I was not popular. I never tried to be. It was easier flying under the radar, because whenever I didn't, something terrible happened.

Like that one day.

My locker was in a newer part of the school called The Annex—a hall with white walls, burgundy floors, and large windows at the end. That day, the windows showcased a stark, cloudy winter sky. The halls were nearly deserted, and I was at my locker, getting ready to go home. I'd just pulled on my coat and was reaching for my hat.

There was this guy. Tall, light-skinned. Close-cut hair. Handsome, but something about him unsettled me. It might have been his piercing light eyes. Or the way he held himself; big and menacing. I always felt like I needed to cover up or hide from him. Fortunately, I didn't usually see much of him, but his locker *was* only several down from mine—so I saw him enough.

That day, he was by his locker at the same time I was packing up to go home. He finished up before I did and turned to leave. But before he departed, he walked over to me, grabbed my front coat flap, and pulled. Then he leered at my chest.

At first, I stood still in shock. There was no way this was

happening. No one would be this bold. We were in a school hallway. What the *actual* hell.

Me: What are you doing?

Him (as if I had the nerve to question him): Looking at your titties.

Me (snatching my coat closed): Don't ever do that again!

Him (indignant): OREO!

An overwhelming plethora of feelings washed over me as he stormed down the hall, muttering god knows what else about me.

I closed my locker. Shaking. Fuming. Confused. Upset. How dare he? He might consider me the class Oreo, but what did that have to do with ogling my chest? I should have yelled back, but I was too stunned. I was too scared.

I was assaulted. And in the moment, I froze, unable to defend myself.

But once I thawed out, a familiar feeling settled in.

Shame.

Shame is hot skin and sweaty hands. Shame is a churning stomach and stinging eyes. Shame is trying to go back and replay the incident with a different outcome, but failing. Shame is guilt magnified times a thousand.

I racked my brain for ages, trying to figure out what I'd said or done to make him do that to me. What made him feel entitled enough to come and move my coat aside? Then to act like *I* was the one who'd done something wrong?

Had I done something wrong? I pop off at the mouth sometimes and say the Exact Wrong Thing. I don't always think before I speak, but I hate hurting people. And often, I feel like if something bad happens to me, surely I've done something despicable to deserve it.

Maybe I should have "acted my color."

★ ★ ★

We doubt. We deliberate. We torment ourselves, wondering if it's our fault. Wondering if we did something to cause it. If we could have stopped it.

We wonder if we were wearing the wrong thing, drinking the wrong thing, saying the wrong thing. Acting the wrong way. Thinking the wrong way. Being the wrong way. Did we do something to lead them on? Did we tease them?

Maybe I was being punished because at the age of eight I watched boys in my class gang up on another girl and harass her every day. I didn't say a word to make them stop. I never stepped up to help her. Or maybe the universe was paying me back because I didn't speak up when a bunch of boys tried, and succeeded, to touch my flat chest when I was in fourth grade. I was horrified. They laughed.

Maybe it was because I *did* act too white. Maybe me being *me* was putting too much of a target on my back. Maybe I needed to change, so I could be safe.

I mean, what if he tried something worse next time?

Next time. Oh, God. Time to backtrack, try to figure out what I did to trigger that behavior, and avoid it. Had I said something to piss him off? Was I acting "fast," even though I tried not to? (And that phrase is a whole other pile of problematic baggage—I see that now.) Was it because I didn't act black enough? Was it because I was the class Oreo? The way he threw that insult out...it was like people who didn't "act right" deserved to be harassed.

I blamed myself. But I blamed him, too. And I blamed the teachers. Why were they never around to help? (In fact, where the hell were the adults in every single incident?) Why did the halls have to be so deserted that day? It wasn't safe. *I* wasn't safe.

I. Was. Not. Safe.

And if I didn't have any idea of who I was before, I was even more lost now.

I was the girl who wouldn't *act her color*, so I didn't feel like anyone would have cared. Maybe they would have thought I deserved it, confirming the thoughts bouncing around in my head, that it was somehow my fault, my fault, my fault.

Shame.

Every single time, every single incident, shame.

I'm supersensitive, but I'm also resilient. I bounce back eventually. I managed to toss that incident to the back of my mind. File it away with the others. After all, it wasn't that big of a deal, right? I hadn't been raped. I hadn't even been groped, exactly. He touched my coat, not me. He just looked. It was fine.

But it wasn't.

Deep in my bones, I knew it wasn't, but I didn't feel like this warranted me making a big deal out of it. Other people had gone through far worse. I didn't want to cause drama.

He never approached me again. In fact, I don't remember even seeing him after that incident. I don't know if I blocked him from my mind, went out of my way to avoid him, or what. High school still wasn't the "best years of my life"…but his absence, among other things, managed to make it bearable until I graduated.

I put it out of my mind. For years, I didn't think of it. I don't know if I suppressed it, or if I simply moved on with my life. Maybe a bit of both. Time passes and slowly heals, bit by bit.

Maybe.

But shame creeps back. What if he did it to someone else?

If I'd told, maybe I could have prevented that. Maybe someone did tell, and that's why he disappeared. I'm honestly not sure, so I try to let it go.

I was fifteen or sixteen when it happened. I didn't know what to do.

I still don't know.

And so the anger comes.

I'm angry, remembering every incident with every guy. All the times guys hit on me, then got angry when I turned them down. The guy who said, "I WILL have you," to me in a threatening way. The guys who never touched me, but told everyone that they did, and more. The one who wouldn't stop until I started crying, then stormed out, as if there was something wrong with me.

And that damn guy, who decided he wanted to have a look at my "titties," so he should damn well be allowed to go ahead and look.

I'm sad, because so many others have had much worse happen to them. Sometimes I feel like my stories aren't valid. I feel like it isn't that big of a deal, and I should be over it…really over it. Not just squashing it away, but truly past it. I feel shame in saying Me Too, when I don't know if the things that happened to me count. In the grand scheme of things, they weren't *that* big of a deal, right?

Except they were. Except they are.

Every instance has had a profound impact on how I move through the world today. How I relate to the media I consume, how I relate to cis-het men. I thought I'd pushed it away, but it made me question my personality for a long time. I felt ashamed of the things I liked. I hid parts of me. I wondered… I still wonder.

I wonder if I'm acting "black" enough. Or…if I'm acting the "right" way. I wonder what will happen the next time someone decides I'm not.

I graduated college. I am no longer living in poverty. I manifested my dream and became a writer. In some ways, I know exactly who Ronni Davis is. In others, I'm still figuring it out. And that's okay. I'm still not sure if I'm extraordinary yet, but I'm sad that my experiences are one way in which I'm "normal."

So, yeah. Me too, me too, me too.

I'm not alone.

Shit.

I'm not alone. (And neither are you.)

★ ★ ★ ★ ★

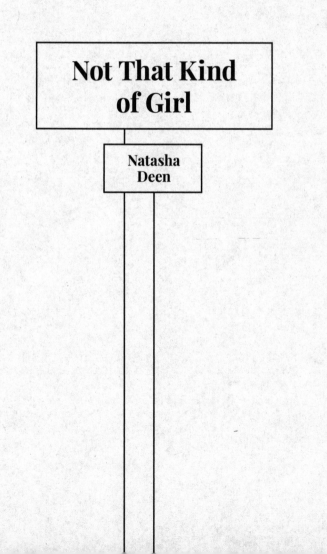

Not That Kind of Girl

Natasha Deen

The days leading up to my entry into junior high school started with the kind of excitement and potential for big, sophisticated happenings akin to the Hollywood movies and teen novels that dominated my free time. Of course, life isn't a movie reel, and my first few months of grade seven involved me explaining—multiple times—that having the same skin color as a kid in the other class did *not* make us siblings. And agreeing with the other girls that having my bra snapped was a compliment (even though I wanted to punch the guys in the face). And repeatedly saying, "Yes, brown people can get tans," and "No, I don't speak another language." The last part wasn't entirely true, but trying to explain Guyanese Creole was a hurdle I didn't have the energy to jump.

Still, I remained hopeful that Hollywood hadn't led me

wrong, and that fabulous, glorious, life-changing things were in store. Topping my hopeful list was the first dance of the year—my first dance as a teenager—and I was ready for it. I'd seen all the movies, and I knew awesome things happened at these events.

I expected my strict, religious parents to put up the first obstacle to the dance. After all, the night could involve *slow dancing*, with my arms around a boy and his arms around me. (The idea of girls slow dancing with girls, or boys dancing with boys didn't blip on anyone's radar—and forget about the segment of the population that preferred a nonbinary classification. This was the eighties, when queer kids wouldn't dare dance with their real crush, and any same-sex slow dance was either a prank—boys—or, in the girls' cases, an adorable and nonthreatening activity to be indulged.)

But my parents, surprisingly, put up no resistance to my request to go to the dance. Perhaps part of it was them trying to acclimate to our new culture and country. Perhaps part of their motivation was that they loved me and wanted their daughter to experience life as she desired. In any case, when the night finally arrived, I teased my hair, hit it with enough hairspray to empty the bottle—not that it helped; ah, the trials of having "ethnic" hair in a white world—and put on my lipstick. I was ready to bust a move, make friends, and rock the world.

My folks dropped me off, and my walk up to the school's main entrance held a foreign, unfamiliar air that felt electric. Then, suddenly, there I was, standing at the doors of the gym, my knees bending in rhythm to the pop song blaring from the speakers, oohing along with my friends at the strobe lights, and convincing myself the DJ wasn't bored out of his mind.

Nope, that was just the look of a grown man astonished and awed to be in the presence of so many extremely cool kids.

One of my friends, who had a mad crush on a boy named Mike*, walked me past him and his friends so I could see what he looked like.

"There he is," she whispered, pointing.

Mike caught the movement. "Do I want to dance?" He laughed. "Not with either of you."

His buddies high-fived him, and I glared in their direction.

We walked away, their braying laughter and jeering taunts following us, and I pondered what it was about hateful, cruel remarks that seems to cut through the noise and buzz of the world. Was it the spite and arrogance in their tone that made them painfully audible above the music and chatter?

My friend and I returned to our spots on the bench, and I tried to forget about Mike and his friends.

Still, thoughts of them clouded my mind. Most of my time in Canada had felt like a boxing match where the referee refused to ring the bell. While I fought round after round, my opponents were allowed to rotate. I fought against feeling invisible when it came to movies and TV that never showed anyone who looked like me. I fought against the assumptions about girls of color. We were—according to some kids and the subtext of certain books—okay to "mess around with," but when it came to "real dating," the preference was the white girl. They were better, superior quality. And I couldn't unhear the subtext—that white girls were pure and valuable. That girls of color were to be used as mere practice tools for the boys.

The thoughts crowded my brain as I stood in the gym, swaying to the music and mentally fighting with Mike. Was his dismissal typical of a boy transitioning from "ew, girls have cooties" to "ah, girls are wonderful"? Was the rejection borne of feeling that my friend and me—both of color—weren't worthy because we weren't white? And if it was the latter, then what should I do if he suddenly decided to pay attention to my friend? Would it be because he had genuinely changed his mind, or because he was practicing?

It wasn't even a half hour into the dance, and I was already exhausted by the weight of my skin color and my gender.

I wanted to talk to my friend about all of it, but she was certain his aggression was an example of the "thin line between love and hate." To her, he was an exemplar of the romance books and movies. Surely Mike was hiding his true feelings, and secretly, he was mad for her. All of it left me just feeling mad, period, but I didn't want to let Mike ruin what could be my Hollywood moment. So I shoved aside my worries and anger, and focused my attention on the night.

The music played, and the teachers patrolled the perimeters of the dance floor, seeking to stop any inappropriate behavior. They needn't have bothered. Though we all dreamed big and talked even bigger, this coed event terrified even the bravest soul. For the first part of the dance, the majority of us stood like sentries propped against the wall, too frightened to be the first to step on the dance floor.

An hour or so into the night, we finally did take to the dance floor. It was the stuff of legend. The dark gym, the thrumming lights, the music blaring so loud no one could hear each other, so conversation consisted mostly of one person shouting to the next, "What did you say?"

Then it happened. The slow song. Everyone scattered. A few brave souls stayed on the floor and danced. Their movements were stiff, their arms board straight, but it was the most grown-up thing any of us had ever seen, and we were amazed.

Emboldened. The next slow dance saw more couples on the floor, then more.

I wasn't one of the popular kids, but I was liked well enough that a few boys asked me to dance. Then Jon★ came and asked if I wanted to join him on the dance floor. I didn't really know him, but he seemed okay. His family was the kind of wealthy that I, as the kid of immigrant parents from a developing country, couldn't comprehend. I found some of his rants confusing but hilarious—what twelve-year-old goes off on the quality of a teak desk versus an oak one, anyway?—but he seemed kind and funny.

Most of all, he didn't make me feel like I was a multicultural prop, and I appreciated that his family's travels around the world meant he didn't ask me things like "What's your first language?"

We danced a few times, and I was intoxicated by the sensation of being a regular, typical teenager. I spent most of my waking life doing two things: feeling different and wishing. Wishing I was the kind of girl who had the cool tote, wore the brand-name clothes, and whose mom let her wear more than lipstick. Wishing I was the kind of girl everybody liked, the kind of girl everyone wanted to befriend, who was confident and kind and smart.

This night, this dance, made me feel like maybe, just maybe, I could fit in.

Here I was, just like on TV. I was laughing with the girls in the bathroom, telling each other, "You look so cute!" and "I love that lipstick!" and then hanging out with boys and joking with them. The hanging out was the best part. Most movies had girl meets boy and then they fall in love, but I was entranced by the stories where the girls and boys were friends. More than friends. *Best* friends, because gender wasn't the thing that mattered or defined the friendship—just like how color shouldn't matter or define a relationship.

Jon could be that friend, I thought. We'd hang out, laugh over stupid things, study together, and share our secrets. How cool was that?

After a couple of dances, Jon asked if I'd like a soda, and I said, "I didn't bring any money."

"That's okay." He smiled. "I'll buy it for you."

Suddenly, the dancing with a neat guy who might be a cool friend seemed to go to a level I didn't quite comprehend. Sure, I was all for boys crushing on me. Who doesn't want to be adored by somebody? But my parents had strict rules.

Boys are awesome as friends.

Have as many as you like.

Hang out with them as often as you like.

But no dating until you're in college. Seriously, college second or third year, and it better not affect my grades, or my eventual entrance into law school, or my future role as a Supreme Court justice, and finally, my position as a Canadian politician.

Thankfully, movies and television had educated me on how to handle this sort of thing. Various scenes rose in my memory and reminded me that just because someone bought a drink for you didn't mean anything other than they were being nice. I mean, I may have been unsophisticated when it came to dating, but I wasn't naive enough to add layers of meaning to what was, at heart, just a nice gesture done on my behalf.

"Thanks," I told him. "I'll pay you back tomorrow."

He plugged two quarters into the machine, and a few seconds later, a can of Coke rolled to the bottom. Jon popped the tab open, handed it to me, and smiled as I drank.

"Aren't you going to have one?" I asked after a couple of gulps.

He took the can from me and took a sip.

And I was officially horrified.

He handed the can back to me, and I had no idea what to do. With my close friends, sharing a drink was no biggie, but I barely knew this guy. My mind spun, trying to think of casual ways to say, "Hey, thanks, buddy. Listen, before I drink, do you have any mono, lip sores, or colds I should know about? And you didn't ask, but for the record, I'm healthy."

What was I supposed to do? To say?

I knew what my parents would have me do. Smack away the offending can. Shoot Jon a glare and demand, "Eh, neh, boi, ya lose ya min'? Me nah gon drink ya' backwash!" Or, to translate from Guyanese Creole into Canadian lingo, "Sir, I am deeply offended. How dare you think I would drink something you have previously drunk from? I do not know you, nor do I agree to engage in actions that would have us sharing bacteria and microbes, and thus, putting us both at risk for infection or illness."

And where was Hollywood in this? I had watched all the movies. Why had the silver screen not prepared me for such a scenario? In movies, the cool girl always ended up with the cool guy. Of course, *of course,* she would share the drink, like it was no big deal.

But movies and books never told me what I was supposed to do in hygienically ambiguous circumstances, and how I was supposed to hold to my boundaries while at the same time not hurting someone's feelings. And that was the worst of it, really—while most girls had been raised to be good girls, I'd been raised to be a GOOD GIRL. Embody the best virtues of Jesus and Christianity—meek and mild, merciful and turning the other cheek. Embody the best virtues of Canadian culture: be respectful and polite. Embody the best virtues of Guyanese culture: everyone is a neighbor, be kind and helpful and turn no one away.

I stared at the pop can, wishing for someone to pull the fire alarm, hoping Jon would say, "Just kidding! I would never do something so wildly intimate as force you to share a drink with someone you've known for thirty seconds," and then buy another soda.

I wish I could remember every moment of that experience and say with certainty that I was brave and secure enough in myself to say, "No, I'm good. If you're cool drinking from a can of someone you barely know, more power to you, but that ain't my thing." Chances are, faced by the crippling desire to not be mean or hurt his feelings or make him feel like he was disgusting—faced with multifaceted societal pressure to *be nice* and *be a good girl*—I subjugated my needs and boundaries in favor of a person I barely knew.

Memory is hazy, but I think I sent up a prayer that I was part dog, and that my mouth thus had the kind of germ-killing ability of my canine counterparts. And then I took a small sip, tried not to vomit it back up, returned the can to him, and said, "Yeah, I'm good now."

We wandered around the school for a bit, then headed our separate ways back to our respective friends. Toward the end of the night, Jon found me for one last dance. When it finished, we walked to a quiet spot in the foyer, and he said, "Will you go out with me?"

"What?" I blinked and tried to register if the thumping I heard was the bass of the music or the banging of my heart.

"Will you go out with me? On a date?" He smiled as though it was a given I'd say yes.

"No," I said, "I can't."

His smile vanished. "What are you talking about?"

"I can't date—I'm not allowed. I'm not—"

I wanted to say, "I'm not that kind of girl," but then I'd have to explain my family's rules, that living in Canada sometimes meant I was "in" Canada but not "of" Canada. I couldn't think of anything further to say, and the entire situation left me feeling humiliated.

"But I bought you a Coke," he wailed. "How can you say no?"

I stared at him, wondering if—hoping—I'd heard wrong. In what world did buying someone a drink mean that person owes you anything but "thanks"? Was I the problem here? Was this yet another one of those moments where being Guyanese left me floundering to understand Canadian culture? Both my grandmothers' marriages had been arranged, and though the husbands' families were poor, I knew the dowry was more than a can of soda that was worth fifty cents.

Regardless, I wasn't agreeing to his request. I didn't like him romantically, but he didn't need to know that, so I told him a different truth. "My parents won't let me date."

"Then why did you dance with me?"

"I'm allowed to dance, just not allowed to *date*." The words were tart and sharp, but I was losing patience. My short stint in junior high had already included scalding looks, cultural misunderstandings, microaggressions, being called a P★★★ and a N★★★★★, people asking if my skin color washed off, if I was brown because I didn't shower, and off-color jokes about the *Kama Sutra*. Now, I was being subjected to someone's *asinine* (emphasis on the "ass" in asinine) idea that I was obligated to him for a date because I ingested three sips of his Coke, and if I was going to have the audacity to say no to him, I needed to somehow justify my behavior.

"This is stupid," he growled. "You shouldn't have danced with me."

On that, we agreed.

He stalked off, and I ran back to my friends. With clipped words and a heart full of confusion, I told them what happened, and asked for their insight.

Many opinions were offered, but in the end, it came down to a single sentiment. Boys were another species. Fun to look at and play with, but ultimately incomprehensible.

The unfairness of it all stayed with me as my mom picked me up, but I didn't tell her what had happened. I wasn't sure if she would go full-on Guyanese Mother and hunt down Jon, or if she'd use my hurt as a reason to not let me out of the safety of the house. All of it left me even angrier with Jon. My parents were strict, and while they embraced many aspects of Canadian culture, they didn't play when it came to certain things. The risk of them further curbing my already restrictive lifestyle was too great for me to tell them what happened. So, I went home and spent a sleepless night, and it would be the first of many sleepless nights, thanks to Jon.

The next morning, I saw him in the hallway. I tried once more to explain that my turning down the date had nothing to do with him and everything to do with my parents' rules, but that was met with sneering contempt. In the end, I gave him the money for the soda—and for one mad moment, I thought he might chuck the coins back at me.

What he actually did was much worse. Every time I saw him after that, whether in the hallways, cafeteria, or class, he glowered at me, then found the nearest person in his proximity to whisper and point my way.

By the end of the day, I was exhausted.

By the end of the week, I was heartbroken.

For me to talk to the other kids about what had happened between Jon and me would have embarrassed him, and I didn't want to humiliate him. But Jon, it seemed, held no such noble convictions, and was only too eager to share his side of the event. His version, of course, painted me in every negative light possible. Manipulative, snobbish, I was the girl who "thought too much of herself," the girl who messed with people's emotions to get what she wanted. Apparently, I was the kind of girl who put a *great* deal of effort and planning into extorting half a can's worth of soda, but no one caught the logic discrepancy.

Indeed, the kids were all too happy to devour his story, to gorge on his toxic gossip. They delighted in coming up and asking me, "Hey, Jon said this about you. Is it true you're a stuck-up b★★★★ and you're better than everyone else?"

When I wasn't subjected to their judgments, I was forced to endure their debates over my decision and his hatred. No one believed my parents wouldn't allow me to date. That was ludicrous! No, the truth must lie somewhere else, and the "somewhere else" was the real reason he hated me.

Theories raged. My standards were too high, and I made him feel inadequate. Sure, Jon wasn't the best, but he was okay—how dare I make him feel inferior? I was too idealistic. So what if I didn't like him, didn't I want a boyfriend? Didn't I want to be like all the other girls?

My cruelty in hurting his feelings meant it was okay for him to despise me. In their eyes, I deserved his hatred.

Among the painful theories—some taking shots at how I dressed, some remarking on the lowly status I held on the popularity scale—there was the idea that I should be flattered that he, a white boy, had asked me, a brown girl, out. More than flattered. I should be *grateful*.

And once again I was in the boxing ring, with no reprieve. I should be on my knees, blithering thanks, because he was gracious enough to see me as an equal. Forget about how I felt; I should accept him and take him into my life because the chances of anyone else ever dating me would be slim.

The theories picked me apart until I was nothing but bone and despair. My defense, that my parents would never allow me to date, no matter how I felt about Jon, brought no mercy. No one believed his hatred could be an overreaction. In the end, everyone seemed to buy into the certainty that I must have done something truly terrible, something neither he nor I would talk about, but something that made me deserve what was coming my way.

And that was one of the things that hurt most: the idea I deserved his emotional violence, that whatever hatred, rumors, or lies he spread about me, somehow, I was culpable in it. I was responsible for it. It was my fault. There was no sympathy for me, no kind word or righteous indignation that this kid felt it was his divine right to wage war on me.

It was up to me to "shake it off," to "let it go," to "accept my part in it." Accept my part? For what? Obeying my parents? For committing the sin of being a kid of two nations and struggling to find balance between them?

Rumors and twisted caricatures of me, carried by whispers and pointed glances, took hold and took on lives of their own. My reputation was forged, locked, and destroyed by half-truths and lies, by stories shared among those for whom gossip was a joyful pastime.

I grew more anxious, more afraid of crowds and people. My days were already spent fending off the racial ignorance.

Now, I had to fight against the assumptions about my gender and sexuality and how I used them. Unfortunately, this new pain wasn't something I felt comfortable sharing with my parents. They already worried I was becoming "too Canadian," and revealing that a boy had turned my life into a living hell because he felt I owed him a date was too big a risk to take.

As the days turned into weeks and months, I grew smaller, found it harder to breathe and spent every hour wishing I could speed up time and be done with all of these people. I hid in my room, retreated to books and TV—fantasy worlds where I could dream that some magical figure would emerge from the mist and take me away from all of it.

Time, however, inched along, and I grew angrier—at Jon, at the kids who locked people in cold cages of assumption and judgment. So, in grade nine, having spent two years as Jon's favorite whipping toy, I lost hold of my patience and my tongue.

He came at me during lunch, and I let him have it. I raised my voice, called him names. It's possible I may have encouraged him to do something anatomically impossible to himself.

I braced myself for the backlash. But instead of starting a brawl, my outburst shut him down. His eyes got wide, and then he mumbled something incoherent and scurried away. The kids around me whooped and hollered, and congratulated me for "finally standing up for myself."

I met Jon's emotional violence with emotional violence of my own and got high fives for my efforts. The whole thing left me feeling sick. Sick of the kids, sick of Jon, sick of myself and how I'd allowed them to push me over the edge.

Jon found me a couple of weeks later.

I braced myself for the onslaught, but instead of rage, I got remorse.

He was sorry, and he felt foolish. When I lost my temper on that day, it woke him up to how unfair he'd been and how traumatic his behavior must have been for me.

I accepted the apology, but it took longer for me to find the forgiveness. Once I did, we were able to have the full conversation about how rejected he felt, how he was certain I'd gone back to my friends and laughed at him. I had a chance to share my hurt and how angry I was that he'd not only tormented me, but brought the entire school into his harassment of me.

By high school, we were best friends, as I'd once dreamed we might be. But the time we spent together was always shadowed by the night of the dance. There were moments I had to remind myself that I'd chosen forgiveness over holding a grudge.

For Jon, it was worse. He carried the shame and regret of his behavior, and it wore on him. He would apologize again and again, and his contrition was a reminder that restraint was a weapon, not a weakness, and that I should never say anything in anger that I wouldn't say in peace.

Over time, our conversation about that night turned into a conversation about his life, and it informed me of the backstory that led to his behavior. It was freeing, finally hearing the confirmation that his actions that night had nothing to do with me and everything to do with him. It was empowering, because I rely on that knowledge whenever people are mean or racist to me, now. I remind myself it's not about me, that for someone to act out with vitriol and to inflict such pain, they have to be in a level of torment and self-loathing I can't fathom.

It doesn't always help. Some days, I'm locked in the unfairness of it all. Some days, I'm raging against the misogyny and institutionalized racism that seem to infect every facet of my life. Some days, I'm just so tired, exhausted to my bone marrow that these injustices continue to be inflicted on women, minorities, LGBTQ2 people, on anyone who doesn't fit the mold.

But I get myself out of it by reminding myself that this life—*my* life—isn't about hoping people treat me well, or that humanity evolves to the point where I can implicitly trust everyone. It's about staying grounded, honoring my boundaries and being aware of when I need to walk away from a situation. This life is about me having the wisdom to know when to let someone go versus when I should hold out my hand and offer grace. In the end, it's not about trusting the world or the people in it—it's about trusting that, no matter what, I'm the kind of girl who'll have my back, even if no one else does.

★ ★ ★ ★ ★

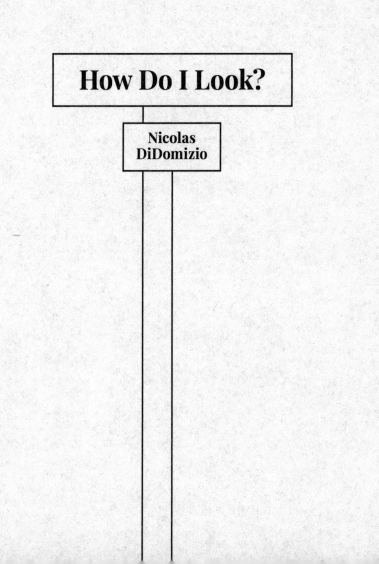

How Do I Look?

Nicolas DiDomizio

When I was a teen, I hated my body: the way it looked, the way it felt, the way it didn't look, the way it didn't feel. The way its curiosities and desires forced me to question everything about myself.

For one thing, I was addicted to gay porn. That was how I chose to frame it back then—the *porn* was gay. Not me! I just suffered from a mild addiction to it. Deep down, I knew this was false, but the lie helped me sleep at night. The era was post–*Will & Grace*, but before legalization of gay marriage. Gayness was still a joke in my tiny hometown—not an identity.

Also a joke? Fatness.

My entire childhood was punctuated by speeches from the doctor about how I needed to lose weight. Fat-shaming comments from family members and peers embedded themselves into my psyche, even when they weren't directed at me. Scientists could have fueled a rocket with the jealousy I harbored toward boys who casually took their shirts off at the pool without thinking twice about it. I begged God to let me trade bodies with one of them.

This prayer was almost answered in eighth grade, when I finally found a diet that worked. I lost fifty pounds in three months. My weight suddenly fell into the "normal" range! My doctor was so pleased. I could fit into medium shirts. I started wearing jeans instead of windbreaker pants. Everyone praised me for my epic transformation, but the cruel plot twist was that I only *looked* skinny. I was still out of shape and flabby underneath my clothes, and at times, this felt like an even bigger secret than my gayness.

Both secrets together meant that I was in a constant state of mental anguish by the time I got to high school. Freshman year, my senior brother would drive me to school every morning with his senior friends. They were cool kids—jocks and bad boys—and their conversations typically bounced between the topics of sports and sex. The latter made my throat burn with shame. According to these guys, the only challenge associated with sex was convincing a girl to do it with you. After that, the hard part was over, and the rest was bragging rights. She had "given it up." You had "scored."

The extent of your bragging rights would vary based on the girl in question. How did she look? If she was *hot*—nice body, pretty face—then you might as well have won the lottery. If she was a "fat chick" or a "butterface," your buddies would probably give you shit for it.

I would always laugh and high-five along with them—desperate for their approval as "one of the guys"—but inside himself to grab my dick, I probably would have said that I'd freak out and tell him to stop.

But I didn't.

Opening my mouth and initiating confrontation would have required a level of self-assuredness that was still light-years out of my reach. Instead, I gripped Shawn's leg in an attempt to draw his attention to what Dylan was doing. I was sure he'd handle the situation for me and say something to Dylan, like, "What the fuck are you doing, man? That's my boyfriend."

But he didn't.

Instead, he leaned over and unbuckled my belt.

I remained frozen. Shawn started kissing me. Dylan kept touching me and Shawn and himself. It occurred to me that they had probably done this before, which made me sick to my stomach. But I still couldn't bring myself to speak up. I feared creating conflict, especially over something as silly and intangible as my own comfort and self-respect. What if it ruined things with Shawn? I had already accepted admission to his school in the fall so we could be together. I didn't want him to think I was some high school baby who couldn't handle his world. I mean, my chance at being "one of the guys" had surely evaporated the second I came out of the closet—but couldn't I at least be one of the *gay* guys? And Dylan was so hot. Who was I to reject him? I should have been thrilled that someone like him was giving me this kind of attention.

So, I forced myself to unfreeze. I kissed both of them back as convincingly as possible. I placed my focus on the familiarity of Shawn instead of the wrongness of Dylan. Eventually, we were all naked. The natural sunlight illuminated parts of my body that had tortured me in secrecy my entire life. Every last nerve ending churned and twisted with discomfort and

I felt a sad empathy for the girls they so casually dehumanized. How could I cast judgment on their bodies when I was so busy hating the appearance of my own? How could I convince a girl to sleep with me if I felt more inclined to identify with her than objectify her?

Coming out of the closet would have obviously eliminated my need to worry about these questions, but that wasn't an option I was willing to explore. Because even if I did—what then? I'd seen enough gay porn to know what men were supposed to look like naked. Bodies like mine didn't exist within the realm of male desire.

I started dating Whitney—a beautiful, carefree junior girl—the fall of my sophomore year. We had a whirlwind romance straight out of a nineties rom-com: handwritten love notes, after-school make-out sessions, late-night phone calls. I relished the proof of straightness she lent to my image, but I also genuinely liked spending time with her. Our relationship felt urgent and real. Even if it was built on a giant lie.

"I think I'm ready," she told me over the phone one night.

My chest sank. "For what?"

"You know what," she replied.

The rest of the call devolved into an awkward back-and-forth about the pros and cons of teenage sex. I tried my best to make her think I wanted it more than anything in the world, while also attempting to convince her it was far too soon. This was a very difficult game!

I hung up the phone feeling dejected and pathetic. Wasn't I supposed to be the one begging her for sex? What kind of guy didn't want to score with his hot girlfriend? I hoped she wasn't asking herself the same questions.

I wished I could at least try. My internet browsing history

consisted exclusively of penises, sure, but maybe a real-life vagina was just what I needed to trigger my latent straightness. I pictured myself successfully having sex with Whitney and then bragging about it to all my guy friends the next day. I would totally reframe it as *me* having convinced *her* to do it—a minor detail that would make a major difference. It would be perfect.

But who was I kidding? The thought of getting naked in front of my girlfriend—or literally anyone—was akin to the thought of jumping off a bridge.

Our relationship went downhill from there. Eventually she left me for a college guy, and I spent the next two years slowly coming to terms with my sexuality—reading other peoples' coming out stories online, binge-watching entire seasons of *Will & Grace* on DVD—until I could finally admit it wasn't just the porn that was gay.

I started talking to a college guy of my own during the spring of senior year.

Shawn and I met online. The infatuation was instant and hopeless on my part. He exuded confidence and charisma—qualities I sorely lacked. But I felt like it might finally be okay to lack them if I could get Shawn to be my boyfriend.

"Wow," he said upon meeting me in person for the first time. I can still picture his mischievous smile in the lobby of his sterile dorm building. "You look so good."

That one little compliment gave way to hours of flirty conversation and boundary teasing upstairs in his room. Eventually we started kissing on his bed. His hands wandered, and I tried not to cringe when they got close to my fleshy problem areas. I was relieved when he stopped to get up and turn off the lights. The darkness calmed my nerves just enough to let him take my clothes off. My heart pounded and pounded and

pounded. We stayed up so late that the sun started to rise and glow through his half-closed blinds. I considered it a small miracle that my body didn't make him run screaming.

Getting naked with Shawn wasn't like jumping off a bridge—it was more like crossing one. Our night together transformed him from a total stranger into the one person I trusted most in the entire world. We started texting and hanging out regularly. I quickly decided we were in love. The thought of undressing around anyone else was still unfathomable, but at least now I knew there was *someone* out there who didn't find me totally repulsive.

I visited Shawn on campus one weekday afternoon that May. His best friend, Dylan, was in his dorm room when I arrived.

Oh my God. I hated Dylan. He regularly cheated on his boyfriend and bragged about how easy it was for him to get laid. But in some strange way, I also craved his approval. He was very good-looking, an Abercrombie model type with a cocky attitude that reminded me of my brother's friends from the car. "You'd be so hot if you did something about your bushy eyebrows," he told me the first time we met.

I promptly invested in a set of tweezers.

Shawn popped in a DVD that afternoon—an indie documentary fittingly titled *How Do I Look* (it was about drag queens)—and the three of us squeezed onto his bed. The lights were off, but it wasn't dark out yet. A familiar glow of sunlight peeked its way through the blinds. The opening credits rolled, and Shawn put his arm around me.

Dylan put his hand down my pants.

I froze. If someone had asked me before that moment what I would have done if my boyfriend's best friend took it self-consciousness. I stared out the window and tried to mentally disassociate from what was happening physically. I knew I had succeeded when Dylan grabbed me from behind at one point and whispered to Shawn, "He has a nice ass." Like I wasn't even there. I was so thankful when the sun finally set.

I drove home that night with a storm of regret raging through my chest, throat, and tear ducts. I hated myself for not saying anything. For prioritizing the pleasure and comfort of these two older guys over my own self-worth. I hated Shawn for not saying anything. I had trusted him to be the gatekeeper of my body, and he casually gave it away to his buddy without even warning me. I hated Dylan for being Dylan. I was acutely aware that this night was just another score to him—another conquest behind his boyfriend's back. I worried he might tell other people what I looked like naked—that I'd be the gay equivalent of him hooking up with a "fat chick," and his friends would give him shit before congratulating him.

I had never wished for a rewind button in my life as much as I'd wished for one during that drive.

So many emotions. Far too many to process in a single night. What would any other guy do? I asked myself. The answer, of course, was that he wouldn't have any of those emotions in the first place. So, I decided to bury them, and cope with the experience by reframing it entirely. As something positive.

I texted my best friend when I got home:

Shawn and I had a threesome tonight!

Most of my friends were girls by then—on the totally opposite end of the "bragging rights" culture that shaped my freshman mornings—but I bragged about it to all of them anyway. They were fascinated and entertained. It was surprisingly easy to distance myself from the reality of the situation and craft a self-empowered narrative out it. *Threesome*. It sounded like something a confident skinny person would do.

But buried emotions have a way of mutating into irrational behavior.

As summer unfolded, I became clingy and possessive over Shawn, demanding his full attention when we were together and obsessively texting him when we were apart. I picked fights with him daily. I couldn't speak up about the threesome, so I spoke up about everything else.

I moved into a freshman dorm room on campus that fall while Shawn and Dylan shared an upperclassman suite. I tried hanging out with them, as if everything was fine, but the sight of Dylan's face made me physically ill. This arrangement lasted for about a week until I convinced Shawn to kick Dylan out and give me his spot, so we could be live-in boyfriends. Dylan was reassigned to a room with a random transfer student. He was furious and stopped talking to Shawn altogether, which felt like a victory of sorts: Shawn had officially chosen me over his best friend.

It was almost enough to reverse the damage from that afternoon. As if such a thing were possible.

Shawn and I stayed together on-and-off for a couple years until we inevitably went up in flames. We fought about everything and nothing. He was a serial cheater. I was naive. He was manipulative. We were the definition of fucked-up.

But when I look back now—over a decade later—and think about the most toxic element of our relationship, I don't think about any of that stuff. I think about *How Do I Look*. That's what feels the most egregious, the most altering, the most damaging.

And it was something I fully participated in. Which I guess is why the experience is still so complicated and difficult and hard to think about. Shawn and Dylan technically didn't force me to do anything. I never verbalized my hesitation or discomfort. Maybe it was showing on my face or in other nonverbal cues, but no one ever expects guys to look for *those*.

And so, for a long time, I just blamed myself for deciding to unfreeze.

But now, I have a little more compassion for who I was back then. My identity was so wrapped up in the struggle to validate myself against the atmosphere of toxic masculinity and fat-shaming and homophobia that defined my childhood. It's amazing I ever made *any* self-respecting decisions.

Sometimes I wonder how things would have been different if I were never fat. Would I have seized the opportunity to have sex with Whitney? Or would I have never even dated her, because my fit body would have given me the confidence to come out of the closet sooner? Would I have been a Shawn to someone else? Would I have been a *Dylan* to someone else?

Sometimes I wonder about those moments in my brother's car. How many of his friends' sexual boasts were just positive spins on negative experiences? Did any of them ever take advantage of a girl's low self-esteem the same way Shawn and Dylan took advantage of mine? How many cues did they ignore?

And I wonder about that afternoon in Shawn's dorm room. How *did* I look? Like someone who was enjoying himself? Or like someone who was twisting and churning and enduring because he didn't believe he had a choice?

If only I had known that I *did* have a choice. Self-worth

isn't something that only straight people with lean bodies are allowed to possess. It's a birthright for all of us. I could have said no. I could have said yes. I could have said *something*. I could have loved my body—the way it looked, the way it felt, the way it didn't look, the way it didn't feel—and given it the voice it deserved.

There is no finish line on the journey to body confidence; it's an ongoing commitment. Since that night with Shawn and Dylan, I've engaged in a few more negative sexual experiences, many positive ones, and lots of self-reflection. I eventually got better at giving my body that voice. I've told guys when I wasn't comfortable. I've changed my mind from yes to no—sometimes even midencounter—and verbalized it without apology. I've felt the power of self-love. I've also felt myself revert back to self-doubt at times. But even on the days I don't totally love my body, I've at least learned to listen to it. And to always trust that its curiosities and desires (or lack thereof) are nothing to be ashamed of.

★ ★ ★ ★ ★

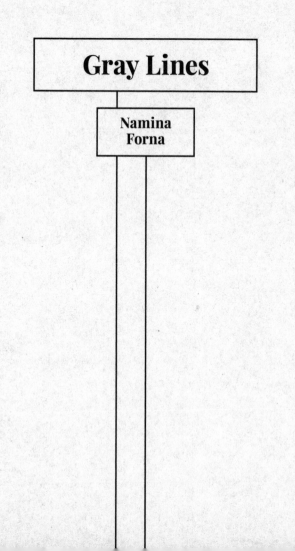

Gray Lines

Namina Forna

I met him at my stepdad's pharmacy. He was tall and lanky, wearing a large golf shirt. He was one of the many vaguely jovial, smiley men that seemed to litter our small, decidedly middle-class Georgia neighborhood. He and my stepdad were deep in conversation when I walked over, list of errands in hand. I stepped aside to wait, but to my dismay, my stepdad pulled me nearer.

"This is the one I was telling you about, the smart one," he proclaimed, much to my embarrassment. My stepdad was one of those people who made friends with everyone he met, but I was the exact opposite.

The man squinted at me. "You sure she's in high school? She looks like a kid."

I hadn't hit my growth spurt yet, so I was only four foot

eleven. With my tiny frame and thick wire-rimmed glasses, people often mistook me for nine instead of fifteen.

"Just turned fifteen," my stepdad replied. Then he gestured at the man. "This is my new customer, Mr. J*. He's a teacher at your school. You can go to him if you need any help."

"Call me Uncle J," the man said, all smiles.

"Okay," I replied, and didn't think anything more about it.

I had more pressing things on my mind. It was my second year of high school in Lithonia, Georgia, and my sixth in America. My homeland, Sierra Leone, was just emerging from its decade-long civil war, a conflict that had devastated my family. Many of my relatives had died, and the ones that survived acquired scars they carry to this day.

I constantly seesawed between worry and guilt. Worry, because my family's situation was still precarious, and some relatives were still missing or held captive in the hinterlands. Guilt, because I'd been one of the lucky ones—I hadn't been mutilated or murdered. I hadn't been forced to become a sex slave like one of my older cousins, who had been captured by rebels when the war hit the capital city of Freetown. The most I could say was that I'd lost some family members, and this made me feel that I had gotten off lightly.

Sometimes I was sad or angry—other times, numb. Most often, however, I just wished I could disappear. That I would fade like a shadow into the walls, and go wherever shadows went when no one was looking.

The other kids at my predominantly African-American high school had no idea. As far as they were concerned, I was an "African bootyscratcher"—the most popular insult for the handful of African immigrants in the school. Even worse, I wasn't a pretty one. My hair was unfashionably short, I wore awful clothes, and, to top it all off, I *willingly* brought library books to class in case I got bored. I was a nerd back when the word was considered a biting insult instead of a badge of honor.

I began noticing Uncle J around school later that week. He was forever strolling the halls, calling out greetings. He was one of those teachers who tried to seem cool, even though he was decades and decades older than all the kids. I reluctantly got into the habit of saying hello whenever I saw him. I wasn't much of a talker and hated anything that brought attention to myself. Still, it was rude not to acknowledge adults, so I always did so quietly—head down, shoulders hunched. I would scurry away at the first opportunity, which seemed to amuse him.

"Where you rushing to?" he'd joke.

I never replied, not that he seemed to mind. He'd pop up every now and then to give me a hug or a quick pat on the back—unwanted demonstrations of affection I bore with quiet resolve. I've never been comfortable being touched by people I don't know, and the hugs were an unpleasant intrusion. As time went on, it almost felt like he was seeking me out. His classroom was next to the exit I used to get to my school bus, so he'd always call out to ask me how I was doing.

"How's it going?" he'd shout. When I mumbled a reply under my breath, too shy to speak out loud, he'd tell me, "I'm always here if you need me."

The next semester, I had a class with him. Within days, he'd made sure it was understood I was his very special favorite. It was the little things—on days when I'd gone to that numb place where all my feelings disappeared and emotions were a distant memory, he'd squeeze my shoulder and give me a pass to spend his class period in the library. I don't know how he sensed it, the numbness—maybe it was a look in my eyes, or the way I kept myself hunched over—but he'd tap me quietly and hand me the pass. At first, I appreciated it—this reprieve from the crushing monotony of the school day—but over time, it became apparent this was another way he could subtly intrude upon me.

When the other students complained about the library passes, he'd turn to them in that jokey way of his. "So, you've finished your work and you're ready to tell me all about it, huh," he'd say.

"No, Mr. J," they'd sigh.

"Well, when you finish your work in advance, you can go to the library, too."

Then, as the other students muttered under their breath, he'd squeeze my shoulder. "It's all right," he'd say into my ear in a low whisper. "They're just jealous because they aren't smart like you."

That was what I hated most. The shoulder squeezes.

Uncle J had very large hands. Even worse, his fingers were long and tapered. I remember because they always seemed to reach near my breasts. Whenever he squeezed my shoulders, I'd stiffen into a board, hoping he'd move his hands away. He never did, and the longer I was in his class, the closer they seemed to reach for my chest, what little there was of it.

I never said a word, though. Back then, I didn't yet understand the American concept of personal space. Sierra Leone is a very touchy-feely place. People hug for what Americans consider an awkwardly long time, and same-sex friends hold hands like lovers while walking down the street. It took me time to get used to the very American idea that you had a circumference of space around you that was yours and yours alone. If I'd understood that more deeply, perhaps I would have been more protective of mine.

Uncle J must have felt my discomfort, but he didn't seem to care. No matter how politely I squirmed or stiffened, he'd always do the shoulder squeezes, the whispers in my ear. As the semester went on, he became bolder and bolder. When I walked into his class, he'd scan me so thoroughly I'd wonder if I'd done something strange to my clothes. Worst were the days when he decided to give me impromptu back rubs because "my posture wasn't correct" and my "backpack had to be hurting me."

He'd give the back rubs to other girls, too. No one seemed to notice how wrong that was, or that he seemed to pay special attention when he did mine.

"You're always so stiff," he'd tell me as he rubbed.

I never replied, never said a thing. Like so many other immigrant children, I was terminally obedient, and feared, above all else, causing trouble to my parents or doing anything that might involve the police. Yes, we were legal immigrants—green card holders and citizens—but I knew, almost instinctively, to always keep away from anything that would lead to legal trouble for my family.

Besides, Uncle J always kept his actions in that middle space where appropriate and inappropriate were a razor's edge from each other. Yes, his touches were uncomfortable, but they were just expressions of comfort from a well-meaning teacher, weren't they? And if I thought his hugs lasted a little too long or he squeezed just a little too familiarly, maybe it was just my imagination. Every touch, every interaction was calculated just so. And I couldn't quite tell the difference because, culturally, I didn't know. I was still trying to assimilate, and certain things about American culture—particularly in the African-American sense—were simply impenetrable to me.

The encounters with Uncle J went on for months, and I

became nervous every time I entered his classroom. I tried to overcome my nerves by telling myself I was too sensitive, that he was just an overly affectionate teacher—harmless in comparison to the other, more predatory teachers at school. The ones everyone said carried on affairs with multiple students. The ones who palmed girls' butts and remarked on how juicy they were.

Besides, this was America. People didn't do those things here, the horrible things I'd witnessed or heard whispered about in Sierra Leone. It was supposed to be safe here.

It was only at the very end of the school year that I finally realized my fears were valid.

On the last day of school, just after the last bell rang, Uncle J called me into his classroom. I was already halfway toward my school bus by then, and all I wanted to do was go home and put the school year behind me. But when I heard my name, my ingrained politeness demanded I go back over to him.

"Have a great summer, Uncle J," I told him quietly.

He smiled at me and held out his hand. "Let me see your phone," he said.

My cell phone was a small blue flip phone, battered from one too many accidents. I wondered why he wanted it, but I handed it over all the same. I remember his big brown fingers pressing the numbers and then his name into the keypad. He smiled down at me in that same jokey, affable way he always did. Then he looked into my eyes.

"Why don't you call me over the summer?" he suggested. Then he added, in a low, but pointed whisper, "Don't tell your dad."

That was the moment I knew for sure. I no longer had any doubts about what it meant when he looked me over in that too-familiar way, or when he invaded my personal space. All

the shoulder squeezes, the back rubs, the free library passes—
this was what they'd all been about. This moment was what
he'd been leading up to all along.

Grooming.

It took my mind only a few seconds to settle on the word
for what he'd been doing. Grooming is the process where a
predator identifies a vulnerable child, then uses rewards and/or
threats to insert himself into their lives so he (*or she*) can have
a sexual relationship with them. I'd learned it a few years back
in one of my middle school classes, but it was a word I'd assigned to the weird men in raincoats who asked you to help
them find their lost puppy, or the shifty neighbor who kept
trying to give you candy. It was not one I'd ever expected to
associate with the teacher who gave me extra library passes and
a hug when I felt upset. It was not a word I'd ever expected to
have use for here in America.

But there it was. Uncle J had spotted a vulnerable, trauma-
tized girl, and had used his understanding of her—*my*—situation to prime me for a sexual relationship.

I don't remember what I said then, but I do remember
scurrying to my bus—remember the fear, disgust and sadness
that surged inside me as I rode home. I never spoke about the
incident to anyone—not to my family, not to my friends. It
wasn't that I was scared, it just didn't seem that big a deal. By
then, I was used to the men at the gas station who leered at
my breasts too long, or the uncle who always seemed very
concerned about testing the shortness of my skirts. This incident was just another in a long line that had started happening the moment I started wearing bras—and, if we're being
honest, well before that.

When the next school year came, I avoided Uncle J and
his hallway studiously. If I saw him anywhere else, I skulked

away or hunched over until I vanished from sight. Eventually, he gave up. I think he left the school sometime before my senior year, but I'm not really sure. I never made any effort to keep track of him, even though I eventually came to find out he had done the same—and worse—to other girls at school.

High school ended, and the encounters with Uncle J faded into the blur of unpleasant incidents I would have over the years with insistent, predatory men. It took me years to acknowledge, however, that it'd had its effects. For one, I couldn't even stomach the idea of dating a man more than three years older than me until my late twenties. Every time an older man expressed any sort of sexual interest in me, I remembered that last day of school, remembered Uncle J leering down at me.

She looks like a kid.

I remembered those words, too.

For years, I couldn't help but wonder if that's what drew him to me—the fact that I was a teenager that looked like a child. Close enough to the real thing to pretend, but far enough away to create reasonable doubt. After all, the age of consent in Georgia is sixteen, and fifteen was so close to that. If a little African immigrant made an outcry, who would believe her? Who would care?

The doubts weren't the only effect of my experience with Uncle J. I've also noticed that I never allow my neck or shoulders to be touched unless it is by someone I truly, deeply trust. I often wear scarves even when it's hot. Even the slightest breeze on that area of my body makes me uncomfortable.

High school is long over, and I'm a much different person now. Sometime after college, I adopted the American spirit of not giving a fuck. Perhaps it was the effect of going to Spelman, an all-female, all-black college where girls were encouraged to be their best, bravest selves. Or perhaps it was just the natural progression of growing up, gaining confidence in myself. It could have also been the therapy that I took to come to terms with my childhood and the things I'd experienced. Either way, I'm quick to tell people no if something makes me uncomfortable now, and I don't ignore that tiny feeling that niggles me whenever something isn't quite right.

These days, I'm much more assertive than I used to be. I speak my mind, draw my boundaries, and know when to walk out if I don't feel like I'm being treated in the best possible way. The years when I was the little African girl who sat quietly in a corner while a grown man made advances on her are long gone, and now, I'm very much an African-American woman who uses my voice.

If there's one thing I want every girl and boy to know, it's this—your body belongs to you, and so does the space around it. If someone ever enters it in a way you don't like, even if it's your parents, relatives, or teachers, you have a right to say no. You have a right to make a fuss and to be loud and embarrassing. Even if it seems silly or there's a chance you might be wrong, do so anyway. The most insidious predators are the ones who operate in the gray lines, the ones who are so subtle, you hardly notice until the line is crossed, and everything becomes black-and-white.

Do whatever you have to do to keep yourself safe.

★ ★ ★ ★ ★

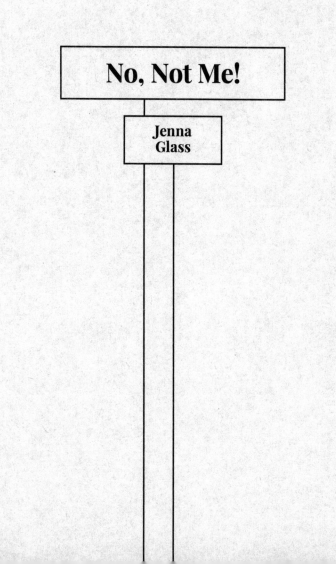

No, Not Me!

Jenna
Glass

I have always thought of myself as a feminist. I remember being outraged as a child when the Equal Rights Amendment was being debated and I was unable to understand how there could even *be* a debate on the subject. I remember my horror when my mother informed me that, as far as the law was concerned at the time, a woman could not be raped by her husband—and my dismay at my inability to convince her that the law was wrong. (We are all, to one degree or another, a product of our time.) But for all of my feminism, I discovered in 2014 that I, like many of my fellow women, was oblivious to just how much discrimination, harassment, and outright assault a woman experiences during her lifetime.

Back before Twitter became all dumpster fires all the time, I spent a significant amount of time on it every day. In theory,

I was on Twitter to promote my books, but I also clicked on interesting links and followed some trending conversations. In 2014—well before the #MeToo movement began—I vividly remember my first encounter with the hashtag that changed the way I looked at my life.

The hashtag was called #YesAllWomen, and its premise was that all women—not just some, not just many, not just most, but *all*—had experienced some form of sexual harassment in their lifetimes. When I saw the topic and got the gist of what it was about, I remember very clearly thinking to myself that *I* had never been harassed or assaulted.

Well, there was that time when I was eight or nine, and that guy flashed me when I was waiting for the school bus outside my apartment building. But that didn't count, really. I was just a little kid, and he was just some random pervert, and things like that happen when you live in the city. It was nothing remarkable, though I supposed it was far more likely to happen to a little girl than to a little boy.

Okay, there was also that time I answered the phone and this creepy dude pretended he was doing a marketing survey and asked me questions about my mom's bra size, which then transitioned into questions about whether *I* was wearing a bra yet. (I wasn't. I was maybe ten or eleven.) But again, that didn't count, because it was just a phone call, and I was just some naive kid who didn't realize that I was talking to a creep. No big deal. Could happen to anyone.

And there was the time I was walking across a crowded train platform on my way home from school and someone reached up under my uniform skirt and between my legs. I didn't outwardly react to it, and I never saw who did it, but to this day I remember the shuddery, skin-crawling sensation of it. Again, not a big deal (at least, I thought it *shouldn't* be a big deal, no matter how violated I felt), because these kinds of things were no more than what I could expect living in Center City Philadelphia—though I doubt there are too many boys who have had the experience of having some stranger's hand thrust between their legs. So while it technically *could* happen to anyone, it was really only likely to happen to a girl.

By the time I remembered this particular incident, I was beginning to get the feeling that maybe, just maybe, I hadn't escaped sexual harassment after all. And then I remembered one more incident, one that left a bigger emotional scar on me than those fleeting encounters with anonymous strangers. (Although clearly one that *still* hadn't convinced me I'd experienced sexual harassment—not until I started reading other women's stories and had my eyes opened.)

It was the summer after my senior year of high school, and my mom and I took a trip to Egypt. It was a great trip (even though we were visiting the Sahara Desert in summer, which I generally would not recommend!), and one of the highlights was a multiday cruise down the Nile. We were on a small ship—the kind where you know everyone on board and have a chance to chat with all of them over the course of the trip—and there was a tour guide on staff. He guided all of our shore excursions. My mom and I both thought he was a terrific guide—knowledgeable and entertaining and personable. It was a magical four days.

Then came the final night of the cruise, and there was a farewell party at which alcohol was served. And our "terrific" guide got drunk. A bunch of us were standing around talking with him, and he asked me about the necklace I was wearing. It was a gold ankh that I had bought at our latest stop, and when he reached toward me, I assumed he was going to look at the necklace more closely. Which he did—right be-

fore plunging his hand down the front of my dress and groping me in front of everyone.

I quickly twisted away, and he got only a brief touch over
my bra, but I was humiliated and horrified. I felt both violated and betrayed by a man I had liked and trusted, and it
was beyond embarrassing to have so many people witness it.
But what happened next was even worse.

The rest of our group—almost all of whom had been at
the party and seen what the guide had done to me—decided
they were not going to tip him. (I don't remember whether
anyone lodged a complaint against him with the tour company—I certainly hope so!) It seemed to me like the only
reasonable decision after what he'd done, but the one person
who saw it differently, the one person who insisted on giving him a tip...was my own mother.

Her argument was that the guide had done a good job up
until the moment he assaulted me, and that it was somehow
"not fair" for him not to receive a tip for the good work he
did. All those other people who had decided not to tip him
were being "cheap" and using his actions as an "excuse" not
to pay the money he was due.

To this day, with my mother long gone, I still feel something inside me shrivel when I remember her *tipping* the man
who assaulted me.

This is not about beating up my mom, though I admit I
was angry with her for a long time. But the truth is, she was
doing nothing more than what society has taught women they
should always, always do: putting a man's needs above everything else. She reasoned that he likely needed that money—
certainly far more than anyone who could afford to take a
cruise on the Nile did—and that being denied his tips might
have caused him undue hardship. And she excused his behav-

ior—in a way that we are also socialized to do—because he was drunk when he did it. Surely a drunken man shouldn't be punished for one small indiscretion. It wasn't as if he actually *hurt* me.

And therein lies the problem. The very problem that originally caused me to think I had not experienced sexual harassment—or worse, *assault*—myself.

The bar for what society as a whole—and women in particular—consider sexual harassment or assault is *way* too low. When I first started reading that hashtag, I thought of harassment as the boss threatening to fire you if you didn't sleep with him, and sexual assault was rape or at least attempted rape. Being flashed or felt up—even multiple times—seemed too "minor" to count. (Even now, I squirm to call what the tour guide did to me assault, even though my logical mind says that's exactly what it was. Though I suspect if it had happened to someone else, I'd have no trouble calling it assault.)

But here's the insidious thing about harassment and assault: the more of it you experience, the higher you mentally set the bar for what "counts." Each of these "small" assaults chipped away at me, at my sense of self-worth and bodily autonomy. They made me feel like prey, with men as the dangerous predators I always had to be wary of. I bought into the idea that these things were all normal, all part of being female. Inevitable. Expected. *Acceptable.*

They are *not* acceptable. Neither girls nor boys should be brought up with the understanding that such things are expected and permissible, and that's one of the great things I think the #MeToo movement is doing for women. Many who've come forward initially did not speak out because they, too, bought into the idea of it being the norm. We are taught to treat these behaviors as nothing more than background noise, like "harmless" catcalls that perhaps we should even consider *flattering*.

The #YesAllWomen hashtag really opened my eyes back in 2014, and I finally acknowledged that I had in fact experienced harassment and assault. And yet when I was asked to write an essay for this anthology, my first thought was that nothing that had happened to me was "bad enough" to bother writing about. Who wants to read a story about someone who was publicly groped and humiliated when other women have stories that are so much more harrowing?

Luckily, I caught myself and realized that I was once again belittling and trivializing my own experience. It's bad enough that there are so many men who seem to think that sticking their hands up teenage girls' skirts or down their shirts is somehow acceptable, or at least excusable. We as women need to reject the concept utterly—and we need to reject it for *ourselves*, not just other people. What happened to me should be considered outrageous and serious and intolerable—even if the man is drunk, or "young and stupid," or "socially awkward" or whatever other excuse he (or others) might give for his behavior.

If we want to reduce the number of more serious sexual assaults, a good way to do it would be to stop tolerating its precursor behaviors. My experiences growing up female in a big city slowly desensitized me to violations of my bodily autonomy to the point where I thought of being groped by strangers as something almost unremarkable (though never unobjectionable). Does it not make sense that the perpetrators would be similarly desensitized? If a man engages in "locker room talk" and no one objects, might he not go on to engage in "harmless" unwanted touching—such as unsolicited back rubs or hand touches? And if those go unremarked, might he not then try more aggressive touching? (I know, I know—#NotAllMen would. But you can't seriously mean that it's only a problem if all men do it, right? Just because every child who hits another child doesn't grow up to be an ax murderer doesn't mean you shouldn't discourage your child from hitting others.)

Every behavior we tolerate, every behavior we fail to call out—because we're trying to be polite, or because we're afraid of the consequences, or because we believe the man "didn't mean anything by it" or was "just flirting"—makes it easier and more likely for him to escalate the behavior. We as a society need to stop the behavior *before* it escalates, instead of trivializing and excusing these "small" assaults. That means calling them out—preferably in a gentle, nonjudgmental way that is more likely to be listened to, though that isn't always possible—even if that makes us uncomfortable. And for women like me, it means taking a long, hard look at what we've internalized as "normal" and realizing that despite how much better things are for women now than they were when I was growing up, we still have a long, long way to go.

★ ★ ★ ★ ★

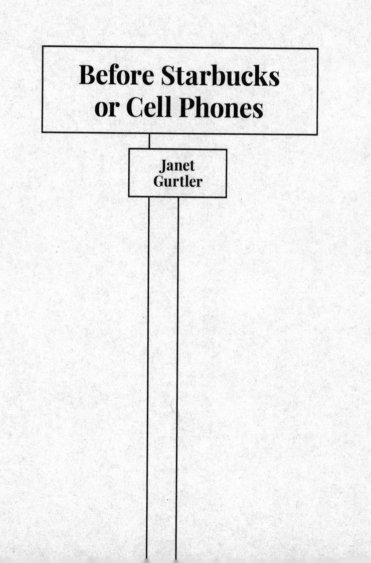

Before Starbucks
or Cell Phones

Janet
Gurtler

I was fifteen when my friend asked me to go to her rape trial with her. She was thirteen when she was attacked. Thirteen when she was raped. The trial itself took a couple of years to make it to court, and by that time we'd started high school and become close. We were probably drawn to each other because we were both a little broken. Our friendship involved a lot of escaping. We drank a lot of alcohol and smoked a lot of weed. We did everything we could to obliterate reality, thinking it was fun and edgy.

But we never talked about how messed up we both felt, or what it was we were trying to forget. We just pretended that all the partying and things we did were cool and normal for teens like ourselves.

When she told me about what happened to her and asked

me to come to court with her, I didn't hesitate. I remember my sense of conviction in that moment. I remember the feeling deep inside my belly. The strength and purity of it. Maybe I wanted to protect her, or maybe in some ways, I did it for myself. I hadn't been raped, but I had put up with my own share of bad behavior from boys.

Either way, I was outraged on her behalf. I was going with her. Standing with her. She deserved justice. I wanted it for her so badly.

I remember my mom initially expressing some concern about me going to the trial, but I was not going to be stopped. She was my friend and she needed me, and of course I had to go with her. This awful, terrible thing happened to her before we'd even met, but it was wrong, and I was going to stand by her side while the court, the law, the judge made it right. I wanted that rapist to pay for what he took from her and what he did. I wanted to find a way to help her.

Of course, I couldn't. Not really. I was too ill-equipped to handle the complexity of what was happening. I wasn't emotionally mature enough. I was still a kid in many ways, and a master at burying my own feelings. I wasn't able to fully comprehend what she was going through or help her deal with it. I don't know that I was able to handle the feelings it stirred in me, either. But I knew I wanted the law to acknowledge that some boys felt they could take things from girls without permission, and that it wasn't okay. I wanted the law to admit that the boys who felt like it was their right to paw at and grab and belittle others were wrong.

I wanted to believe that we were not objects. I wanted to fight. But I didn't know how to express any of that. So I went along with her, and I hoped—no, *believed*—she would prevail.

Like most thirteen-year-old girls, my friend was a virgin when she was raped. Her family had been on the way to their vacation cottage. She got in a fight with her dad (as teens are wont to do), and he kicked her out of the car about a mile from the cabin and made her walk the rest of the way, to teach her a lesson. Dads did stuff like that back in the '70s and '80s—he had no reason to believe that she wouldn't be safe, after all.

Instead of that intended lesson, this young girl was picked up by a group of people who were drinking and doing drugs. They gave her a ride, and then one of the men raped her.

I stood in the courthouse bathroom with my friend and her mom on the day of the trial. Through the walls, we heard the rapist in the men's room next door, throwing up. Presumably from nerves. The sound pleased me. He deserved to be sick to his stomach about what he had done.

But when he got on the stand, we were forced to listen to the rapist's lawyer telling the judge many examples of how he'd turned to Jesus, become a better man. As if embracing Jesus now gave him a pass for what he did back then. When she was thirteen.

Days later, after the hearing, I received a tearful phone call from my friend. A verdict had been reached.

The rapist was found innocent.

The very thought of it was horrifying. The room spun around me as I registered her words. My brain fought to comprehend what was happening, and time seemed to stall. I remember listening to her cry, and not being able to find any words to fix her. There weren't any. I was overwhelmed and completely unable to help her process the enormity of what happened to her. Again. And yet, even then, I knew I felt only a small part of her powerlessness. I absorbed only a small part of the additional trauma this caused her.

She later told me that the judge believed she had sex with the guy to get back at her dad, and then later got scared and lied about being raped.

She was thirteen years old.

She was a virgin.

She was innocent.

We crept through the aftermath of that phone call. It's a haze now, what happened next. We gradually stopped talking about it. I don't remember when, exactly. Our friendship had its ups and downs, and then we drifted apart. Eventually, I moved away and lost touch with that friend—as happens when you move around a lot—but I will never stop caring about what happened to her. I will never forget what happened when she tried to tell the truth.

Telling the truth was hard. That much I did know. Because sometimes the truth about young people and sex makes other people super uncomfortable. And people don't like being uncomfortable. In the time I grew up, we didn't talk to our parents about sex. At least I didn't talk to mine. It was a deep, dark subject that I was sure they knew nothing about. How could they, when they were so old? But this sex stuff—it was spilling out everywhere.

Sexual harassment was served all around me in my teen years. It was a dirty secret in my middle school. I had a seventh- and eighth-grade teacher who was the worst sort of predator and bully. He was eventually arrested for molesting young boys, but we didn't know that at the time. Rumor has it that the allegations and charges against him eventually led to his suicide in a jail cell.

I remember him barging into the girls' locker room after

gym class when we were stripping out of our gym clothes. He walked in when girls were in various stages of being undressed. I remember the sickening feeling and overwhelming horror that he had invaded our private area, and the way he sneered at us. His words were biting and callous and pierced our skin, as I'm sure he intended them to. I remember he laughed the kind of laugh that rings of absolutely nothing funny and told us all we had nothing interesting to look at. I remember feeling embarrassed and belittled. Most of us cowered and covered ourselves as this authority figure, this man who was supposed to be our mentor, told us we shouldn't even bother covering up, because there was nothing to see. They felt shameful, his words. He lobbed them at us and seemed to take pleasure in our discomfort.

And then he strutted out of the room and left a dark cloud in his place.

I think we all quietly dressed and got out of there. I don't think we really talked about it after. I don't know that any of us ever told our parents. I certainly never told mine. It was just one of those things that happened. One of those secrets.

There were other things that "just happened" in that same school around that same time. Some of the eighth-grade boys had somehow come up with this "game" of chasing girls at recess and after school. That in itself was fine—it was what they would do when they caught us that was the problem. They would stick their hands up under our shirts. Feel our bras. Grab at our boobs.

It wasn't all the boys who were involved, but it was the boys who were considered popular. And popularity is a very, very valuable commodity to middle school kids. And the part that I find almost as horrifying now, reflecting back on that time in my life, was that the girls played a part in it, too, because somehow it became almost a badge of honor to be one of those girls who were chased. Like we were the chosen ones. Like the boys felt up only the girls they believed were *worthy* of their sick harassment. The popular, pretty, wanted ones. And we girls kind of bought into it. I think we all knew it was wrong and not good for anyone, yet it was an almost prideful complaining amongst the "victims." We were young and naive, and we were learning all sorts of bad lessons.

We didn't tell. Not yet.

Then something else happened to me, with those same boys.

The Other Thing is something I've thought about a lot lately. I guess I've thought about it more than I realized, because I wrote a similar scene about it in a book that was published in 2009. In that book, the sixteen-year-old main character deals with her trauma by drinking to forget.

Funny. I did a lot of the same thing as a teen.

In that book, the girl ends up committing suicide.

But I'm still here. And now I'm telling the story.

None of my memories from that night are crystal clear, because it happened a long time ago. But I remember those three boys. I remember the bruise on my hip. Oversized and ugly—exactly how I felt at the time. I still feel guilty, as if I somehow did something to cause it. As if I invited it to happen, and that it was my fault.

That night, those cool boys from my middle school found out where I was babysitting from a friend (who turned out to not be a friend at all—another story for another day). Two of these boys had "girlfriends," and one of the girlfriends told them where I was. My supposed best friend.

I think I knew from talking to a friend that they were trying to find out where I was babysitting, but there was no warning in real time that they were coming. Remember, this was before cell phones and texting and Snapchat and always being available to each other. We used landlines to talk. That was it. So I was on my own at the house, downstairs watching TV while the kids slept upstairs. I remember that I wasn't overly surprised that they showed up, and I later found out that my friend had given them the address.

They stormed inside, and the three boys turned into one monster, pushing each other on. The monster had six hands. It was angry. Demanding. Six hands grabbed at me. Six of them.

"Get her. Grab her." They spoke in short, terse sentences. I remember my fast breathing. My head feeling fogged. I couldn't believe it was happening. My mind fragmented, as if I was already compartmentalizing the event, even as it was happening. I was already in denial. I was already shamed and taking blame.

I understood in some way that what they were doing was wrong. But it confused me, too. Was this the kind of attention I was supposed to want? Was this what being desired looked like? Why were they doing this to me; what had I done to deserve it? It must have been something.

The six-handed monster tried to go a little further than just feeling my boobs, until I ran from them and locked myself in a bathroom. That's when I got the giant bruise on my hip—when I slammed into the sink and pushed the door closed behind me.

It was a tiny bathroom off the living room. I leaned on the sink, sweat on my forehead, panting and wishing they'd leave. I didn't cry, not yet. I remember hearing them talk. Laugh. I remember they smoked a cigarette in the living room while I hid out in the bathroom.

Finally, what felt like hours later, they left.

I crept out of the bathroom and panicked at the smell of cigarette smoke, and raced to open the patio door to let fresh air in. I remember the terror in my soul that the couple I was babysitting for would smell the cigarette smoke in their house and tell my parents. I think I checked on the kids upstairs, but they were still sleeping.

When the couple came home, I wanted nothing more than to get out of that house. I rushed away with downcast eyes.

And went home.

I never told my parents what happened. I did talk to my friends the next day. I think I showed a couple of them the bruise. But we didn't discuss it much. It was just one of those things that happened.

When writing this essay, I contacted one of my old middle school friends, to see if she remembered what the boys used to do to us in eighth grade. And to ask her how she felt about it now, as a grown woman.

This is what she wrote to me:

One thing that stands out was the idea that it was our fault, what happened, and that we couldn't tell anyone because we would be blamed. I'm not sure if you remember this, and I hope it doesn't bring up anything really bad for you, but there was a time when you were babysitting, and I found out some of the boys were going round there. The word *rape* wasn't used; I can't remember exactly what was going to happen. I do remember we called your house to get the number of where you were, but your dad wouldn't give it to us. We should have been able to say, "But Mr. MacLeod, some boys are going round to do bad things," but then, it seemed like saying that would get you in just as bad, or even worse trouble from your parents than if the boys attacked you.

And it was true. My dad was an authoritative parent. Girls phoning with dramatic pleas to reach me, to warn me, wouldn't have made him divulge anything. And afterward, we were all too afraid to say something, because we thought we were somehow to blame, too. We didn't want to get caught being bad.

I do remember that my friend, the one I spoke to recently, was very upset by what had happened to me, way back when. Just as clearly as I remember not wanting to dwell on it, talk about it, or deal with it. When I contacted her, she expressed how upset she had been at the time. She even apologized to me for not saying anything back then. Of course, I didn't blame her. I didn't want to talk about it. I didn't want her to say anything. We didn't talk about those kinds of things with adults.

I just wanted it to go away.

But does it? If you don't deal with it?

I don't know. I doubt it.

I do know I was never invited to babysit at that house again. And to this day, I have a continued unease about teen babysitters, and never hired teen babysitters for my own child. Not once when he was growing up.

One of the girls at school ended up telling a male teacher what was going on and what had happened to me. I think it was the same girl who told the boys where I was—the one who turned out not to be my friend. This teacher, though— he was one of the good ones. (Trust me, even then, there were good men, too.) This teacher called in the group of girls who were being harassed to find out what was going on. He asked us questions. I remember the shame and downcast eyes when he asked about the Other Thing that happened to me.

I remember begging him not to tell my parents, as if I was the one who did wrong. We were all worried that we would be punished, and we didn't want to get the boys in trouble. As far as I know, this teacher didn't tell. It was a different time, and we absolutely did not want him talking to our parents. I do remember sensing how conflicted he was, though. He cared, and he was angry that we were being harassed. I sensed that, too. But he honored our wishes. He spoke to the boys, and the "game" stopped.

And then he let it go.

Of course, this wasn't the first time I was exposed to sexual harassment. Quite literally the first time I was exposed was when I was flashed by a stranger when I was about six or seven. Too young to understand completely, but not too young to know it was wrong that some man showed me his penis. Not too young to feel very sick inside about it.

The next time that stands out wasn't horrible, not in comparison to so many other stories. But it made an impact on me. It also hammered into me the reality that I could be shamed merely for being.

For being a girl.

I was eleven or twelve and starting to develop breasts. I may have started to notice boys, and maybe kissing seemed pretty intriguing. But that was about it.

That day I wore jean shorts that were probably too small because I was growing, and a tight red T-shirt I was also outgrowing. It was itchy and tugged at my neck. It was a hot summer day, and I was alone, on my bike, heading to a friend's house. I was a kid just being a kid, and I stopped for some reason on the street, one leg on the pedal, one foot on the road. I heard voices yelling and looked up. A group of construction workers working on a nearby house were staring at me. Calling things to me. About me. Things that were "dirty." I can't remember exactly what they said, but I remember the feeling in my stomach. The fear. The shock. And quickly, the shame stains on my cheeks.

To them, I was not a person. And let's hope they truly didn't know how young I was. But even if they had? Was it okay to yell things at me, no matter what my age?

There is far more awareness today about boundaries and consent than there was when I was young. When I was growing up—before social media, before Starbucks—slut shaming was a thing. The boys who had lots of sex were often considered the studs. The girls who had sex were sluts.

Girls were taught that we are objects. Objects to be used. But we are not.

I don't have a daughter, but if I did, I would want her to have control over her own body. I would speak to her about consent. I had those conversations with my son while he was growing up, but lately, I've worried I didn't do it enough. I still send him texts sometimes, about consent and respect. He probably rolls his eyes at his wacky mom, but he seems to get it. I hope he does. I worry and I probably repeat myself. Maybe my tendency to say things over and over is not necessarily the best way to be heard. But we need to keep talking about the hard stuff. And we need to listen. We need to hear from survivors. We need to work toward making this world a place where young people will be able to say with confidence, "NOT ME. It never happened to me."

It's what we all deserve.

★ ★ ★ ★ ★

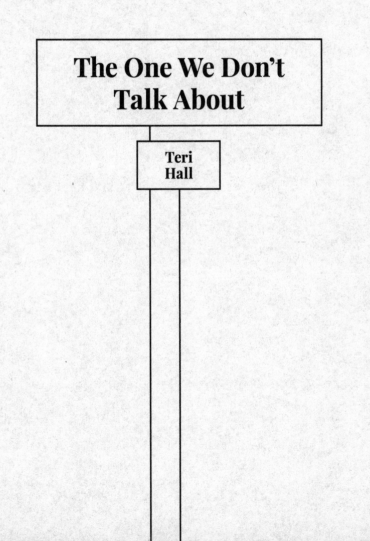

The One We Don't Talk About

Teri Hall

I was three and a half years old when I discovered that there is no god. At least not a god in which I could believe. That year, my father received an adult baptism in a Methodist church (don't ask me why—I have no idea, especially since our family was not what anyone would consider religious). The church was in the small town where I spent my entire childhood, living with my mother, father, and sister in a modest ranch-style house, attending kindergarten through high school with the same thirty-odd students in my class. We weren't rich, but we weren't poor, either. My mother was already a ghost of herself at twenty-eight. My father was evil.

I remember a strange sort of hopefulness blooming in my toddler heart the day of his baptism, as I watched him walk to the baptismal font, an anticipation that built with each step he took toward the minister. I knew who my father was, what he did. And I had some vague understanding that a God with a capital G should strike him down for it. But when the minister touched my father's forehead with the holy water, *nothing* happened. He didn't spontaneously ignite; no flames licked eagerly at his face, consuming him to make him pay for his monstrous actions. The people of my small-town congregation simply clapped and smiled; the minister smiled, too. And that tiny blossom of hope shriveled in my heart, replaced by the coldest, most frightening realization:

Nobody was going to save me.

I was three and a half years old, and god did not save me.

That day, I knew for certain there was nobody more powerful than my father. He could do whatever he wanted. He was invincible.

I found the program for that baptismal ceremony years later, while going through some of my mother's papers. The date on it confirmed how old I was that day. I think about that every time I see a three-year-old now, being led somewhere by a mother's hand, or playing in a park, or crying in a store. I think about how much a three-year-old can know. At that tender age, I had already been abused by my father enough to fear him, enough to fervently wish that some magic god would smite him. Enough to have my heart broken by the realization that that sort of god didn't exist, and that I was alone.

I've had people tell me I was wrong about the god part, though nobody has ever convinced me of it. I certainly *wasn't* wrong about the realization that I would not be rescued. For years—for the next *decade*, in fact—after that day in church, my father did whatever he wanted to both my sister and me.

Incest. It's a #MeToo sort of thing for certain, isn't it? But while we are hearing (thank goodness) more and more people speaking out against abuse of all kinds, we don't hear too much about incest. It's a gritty little secret that families keep, the one that the women (and men) who have lived through never share with anyone. Its victims are well trained. We've been shown that we must keep our silence—shown by our mothers, our grandmothers, our aunts. Incest is the one kind of abuse that we still just don't talk about. And so the sick, black malignancy continues to grow, coiling forward through generations, thriving in the dank, fecund ground of secrecy. Who knows why it exists, this deformed, malevolent growth. But it does, and it feeds on children.

In our small town, nobody locked their doors. There was one grocery store and a drive-in burger place. My father's mother and stepfather—they called him Shorty—lived just a mile away from our house. I know now that Shorty molested my father's two sisters—my aunts both confirmed this to me when I was an adult. I'm guessing that he also abused my father, burying deep an ugly seed that would later spring to festering life when my father was an adult himself. But Shorty's secret was carefully kept within the family. I was warned at a young age, by my mother and my grandmother, never to be alone in a room with him. "You come on in the kitchen with us," they would say at family gatherings. They *knew* what he was. They knew, and yet they kept silent.

I wonder now if they knew about my father, too. When we sat down together for those holiday dinners—were the women all aware that there were *two* pedophiles at the table? Not just one?

As I grew, I missed a lot of school. The stress of being an incest victim takes a huge toll; my childhood was filled with excruciating, mystery stomach pains and malaise. My mother often sympathized, but she never asked me what was wrong.

Clearly, she didn't *really* want to know. And guess who was allowed to come "check" on me when I was home sick from school, and my parents were at work? *Shorty.* Though my grandmother and my mother had warned me to avoid being in a room alone with him when I was a very young child, they did not hesitate to allow him access to me at age seven, and thereafter. Had they simply forgotten those earlier, whispered warnings that came from their own lips? Were they hoping he had changed? I guess they were willing to take a chance on that.

And so, I went from being molested by not just one man in my family, but by two. And I was shown, again and again, how little I meant to the people who were supposed to love me and keep me from harm. I was never sure why it was this way; I understood only that I would never be important enough to protect. I quickly came to believe what I was told in every way imaginable—that I didn't matter.

Once, when I was around nine, I came up with the brilliant idea to lock the doors to stop Shorty's visits. By that time in my life, even considering doing this—an act of resistance— was daring and brave. I'd been thoroughly indoctrinated as to how I should behave: be quiet, be compliant, and don't rock any boats. My mother made it clear. Even my sister made it clear. They were both so afraid. But I was tired that morning, and I had a fever, and I couldn't bear the thought of one of Shorty's visits. So, I locked the doors and waited, my fingers literally crossed.

I lay on our sofa under an afghan, hiding, even though the curtains were drawn and there was no way he could see through walls. I remember hearing the crunch of gravel under his car's tires as he pulled into our driveway. I heard him try the doors, front and back, heard him call my name. And then, he drove away. He just drove away! I felt such hope that day, such optimism for the future. I had found some power.

But that evening, Shorty came back and spoke with my mother. He told her he'd been unable to check on me because the doors were locked (so *strange*, he said; he'd been *worried*). My mother promptly gave him a key to the house.

After he left, I ran sobbing from the room. My mother didn't follow to see why.

There were no telltale signs of abuse, no broken bones, no bruises. Still, people—teachers, relatives, friends—knew something was wrong. I couldn't pretend as well as my sister and my careful mask occasionally slipped. Sometimes, someone would make a vague inquiry.

Everything okay?

You seem sad.

But they never asked if anyone was hurting me. They never said, "Do you need help?" They never pressed. And when you're already convinced you mean nothing, or that somehow what's happening is your fault—or that if you reveal anything, you, or someone you love, will pay dearly—you're not going to assume it's safe to confide.

Finally, at thirteen, I couldn't endure another minute. I gathered all my courage and told my mother what was happening. She looked at me for the longest time with a blank expression, and then assured me through her tears that she would ask my father if it was true when he got home from work.

That's how powerful he was perceived to be in our home.

Here's the thing: mothers can love you, or at least *think* they love you and still not protect you. Same with grandmothers and aunts and even uncles. Maybe they don't know how they would be able to care for you if they changed the way things are. Maybe they're scared; maybe they're cowards. Maybe for my mother, the world back then was different than it is now, and there was truly nowhere she could have gone.

Maybe there was just something *wrong* with my mother, something missing from her that was as crucial as what was missing from my father, something that allowed her to let her own daughter be used and abused and worn down to an empty, sad little remnant of what she could have been. Perhaps there was something broken inside her that let my mother live day after day, year after year, in a small three-bedroom house, and claim she didn't know what went on there.

But here's another thing. It's not like that now. Not for you. You don't have to wait for someone to save you, if you're going through anything like I went through. You can save *yourself.* You can reach out to people who know how to help.

Don't keep that secret. Don't believe that you should. Don't believe that you're worthless, that you don't matter, that you're crazy, that you deserve what you get. Don't believe *anything* they tell you, with their words, or in other ways. It's all a lie— just like it's a lie that your abuser is all-powerful. And don't worry about getting people you love into trouble. Start with loving *yourself,* if you can.

Believe *this*: You do matter. You are the only one of *you* there is, and you are beautiful and good. And there are people out there who know this. There are people out there who know how to love you, and who *will* protect you. You can get out whole, or at least whole enough that you can heal. All you have to do is call a number.

If you are living through anything like what I lived through, you need to call 1-800-656-HOPE (4673).

Call *now.*

Can we end incest? I don't know. Can we break the chain of this secret disease, stop it from happening at all? I don't know. Can you, the person reading this now, the person being abused by someone who is supposed to love you the most, break the pattern for *you*?

YES.

You *can*. Speak out. Call that number and tell the person who answers the telephone what is happening to you. They are out there. They are waiting for your call. They want to help you. They *will* help you. But first, you have to help yourself.

First, you have to pick up the phone.

★ ★ ★ ★ ★

RAINN: Rape, Abuse and
Incest National Network centers.
rainn.org

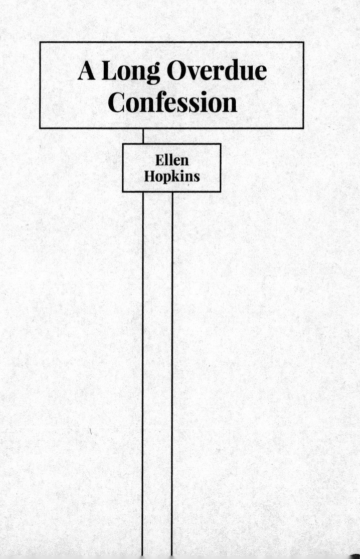

A Long Overdue Confession

Ellen Hopkins

As the #MeToo movement kicked into high gear and people began to share their stories of sexual assault and harassment, many of us were forced to confront painful chapters of our personal histories. And, as questions about the legitimacy of some of the accusations arose, we also had to examine the veracity of our own recollections, especially if the episodes occurred a long time ago.

I've wandered this planet for more than six decades, and so have experienced sexual harassment many times, ranging from so-subtle-as-to-make-me-question-validity to touch-me-again-and-you'll-be-sorry. As an adult, I've been able to craft appropriate responses, or at least I consider them fitting. But thinking back to my teenage years... Well, I could handle overt provocations, but I was ill-equipped to deal with more artfully coercive encounters.

My upbringing, of course, played a role in that. I was adopted at birth by an older couple. My father was seventy-two, and my mother forty-three, when they brought me home to a relatively affluent neighborhood in Palm Springs, California. The family dynamic, as you might guess, was interesting, to say the least. Bear with me here, because everything I'm about to write plays into the ultimate result. It's probably not what you think.

Daddy was born in San Francisco in 1883, the son of German immigrants who arrived with very little. Yet he lifted himself out of poverty, through intellect and hard work. In the early part of the twentieth century, he built a steel company, which became quite lucrative during World War II. He was married to his first wife, the true love of his life, for forty years. Margaret died from lung cancer, the unfortunate victim of the tobacco industry's early propaganda efforts. Her death affected him deeply.

My mom was born in 1912, and the Great Depression defined her life. Her family was also poor, and after the crash, it was all they could do to survive. Though she never provided details, Mama alluded to some of the things she was forced to do as a young woman simply to afford food. Determined to rise above it, she studied nursing and served as a WWII Gray Lady. Afterward, she worked as a private caretaker for a man until his death.

In need of a job, she applied for a receptionist position at a steel company in San Francisco. The owner, my father, was lonely. She was lonely. They married a year later, perhaps more out of desperation for companionship than love. That is not my judgment to make. Daddy and Margaret had never had children, but even late in life, he wanted a family. So he and Mama adopted me and, two years later, my little brother.

It was no secret that Daddy was the undisputed king of his castle. He controlled the finances, paid all the bills. Mama wanted for nothing, but possessed little autonomy. She and I had horses, and often took long rides together. We talked on those trails, and sometimes she shared her disappointment that she'd always had to rely on others for life's necessities. She was bright, and once upon a time had dreams of the theater. One of her greatest memories was performing Shakespeare with a troupe in Ashland, Oregon. It struck me then, even as a child, that I wanted to be in control of my journeys.

There were drawbacks to having older parents. Recreational pursuits were limited, as my father walked with canes. Likewise, extracurricular activities, because Mama's night vision was poor. We didn't ski or hike or ride quads (all things I pursued with a passion later in life), and movies were matinees. But overall my childhood was happy, if sheltered. We lived in a beautiful home, and summered at Tahoe. I went to an excellent private school through the eighth grade. Our family attended church every Sunday. I took piano, dance, and vocal lessons.

Still, in the back of my mind lived a little voice, and it insisted something must be wrong with me, or why would my biological parents have given me away? Logically, I understood that unmarried mothers in the 1950s often gave their babies up for adoption, but emotionally, it was impossible to accept.

A particular incident stands out even now, close to six decades after it happened. The adoption was private and arranged by a doctor friend of my father's. He came to visit one afternoon when I was four or five. My parents and he had gone out on the patio to talk. I eavesdropped and heard the doctor remark, "Ellen's mother has another daughter, and she is the prettier child." That might not be word for word what he said, but that was my takeaway.

It branded me.

For much of my childhood, I struggled with my weight and body image. My best friend and I were always trying the latest fad diets. From SlimFast to a Cool Whip fast (!), none of them worked. The boys in my class nicknamed me "Elsie the Cow," and honestly, though it hurt, I couldn't blame them. The girls, I'm afraid, weren't much kinder. A fortunate growth spurt soon changed that, but it took some time for my brain to acknowledge it. When I looked in the mirror, I still saw the chubby girl, hungry for positive attention.

The summer after eighth grade, we moved north to the Santa Ynez Valley, which is just east of Santa Barbara. Starting high school where I knew exactly no one was both good and bad. I had no friends, but I had no baggage, either. No one called me Elsie, or looked at me like that *should* be my name. In fact, for quite a while no one looked at me at all. I could have been furniture. That felt normal, but I decided that wasn't what I wanted.

I pulled myself out of my shell, worked hard to develop a positive outlook. Eventually I found friends, a decent crowd to run with. Well, *decent* is a relative term, I suppose. Let's call it a rebel crowd. We were anti-war (Vietnam), anti-Nixon, and pro-weed, at a time when weed wasn't legal. Sometimes we ditched school in favor of the beach, and once I got my driver's license, I was often behind the wheel.

My father died not long after that, and my mom melted down. I did my best to help her through the legal morass of probate, a poorly executed trust, and IRS woes. But those very adult problems were beyond my ability to mitigate. It hurt to watch Mama suffer, and she truly did. Even more painful was the fact that her resulting depression caused our communication to crumble. She'd been a great mentor before, but no longer. We didn't fight or argue—we just quit talking. She also pretty much freed me to come and go as I pleased.

Boyfriends? I had them. My strong moral sense insisted I wanted love before sex, and I tried to stay true to that. But honestly, I grew bored easily. I'd stay with a guy for a few months, only to find someone else who interested me more. In retrospect, I see I was craving the attention I lacked when I was younger. But I think I also feared hanging on to a relationship too long would mean relinquishing the control I felt compelled to maintain.

Regardless, I liked men. A lot of my friends were male. That didn't always mean hooking up for sex, however. I simply preferred their company to that of most of the girls I knew. Hanging out with the guys was drama-free, and there was no jealousy or competitiveness on display. They didn't worry about manicures or makeup. We could go camping or fishing or dirt-bike riding. We had fun. In contrast, with notable exceptions, my female classmates seemed stuck-up and petty. I developed only a few close friendships, so I never really discovered true woman-woman bonding until later in life.

This feeling was exacerbated when the boyfriend of someone I considered a good friend attempted to rape me.

"Audrey" and I were with him at a downtown event. He was driving, and she had to be home before I did, so he dropped her off first. Then, rather than take me home, he detoured down into the riverbed and parked. He was a brute, much bigger than I, and intent on assaulting me. Fortunately, he was so large that he couldn't move very quickly. When he tried to pin me, I kicked him in the appropriate place and was able to escape. It was a very long walk home, but I managed it.

The experience shook me. Not only the act itself, which was terrifying and came as a total shock. I mean, I knew the guy, not to mention the fact that he was going out with my bestie. How could I have been so blindsided?

I thought Audrey should know—after all, if he tried it with me, why wouldn't he do it again to someone else? But when I told her, she cut me off, called me a liar, and refused further communication. I was astonished by her reaction—I was the injured party, and the physical damage could've been much worse. Why would she blame me?

As a quick aside, the majority of sexual assaults go unreported, and often it's because the victims are afraid people won't believe them, or that they'll be blamed somehow. I never reported the attempt to the authorities—nothing happened, really. So what was there to prove? And, after the way Audrey reacted, I divulged the story only to a few other friends, people I knew would trust my word.

That was a very long introduction to the story I want to profess. I've never shared it before, mostly because I knew I'd have to confront my own complicity. Writing it here, however, has allowed this softly complaining ghost out into the light of day, and for that I'm grateful. It is rarely wise to keep a genie bottled up too long.

I've had only one real nine-to-five kind of job, and that was the summer after I graduated high school, when I went to work for a small company that manufactured faux stained-glass panels and lamps. They were made with resin, which was poured into molds. The plastic was liquid, and a catalyst mixed into it made it harden, releasing a lot of heat. For a summer job, it was hot, messy, and dangerous, as the catalyst was an abrasive chemical that could cause burns if it came into contact with the skin. But the factory was a creative space, and I loved getting paid to make beautiful things.

The business was owned by two men, both of whom spent many hours every day on the premises. "Greg" was well into middle age, and he was kind and patient as he showed me how to accomplish my assigned tasks. "Jim" was thirty-five, extremely handsome, and funny. Not to mention flirtatious. I was eighteen, completely into the range of "consent," and the attention of an older man made me feel desirable and sophisticated.

He'd take me to lunch. Ask about my life. Act like he valued my opinions. He made me laugh. Made me think. Made me feel important. The first time he kissed me, I was over the moon. The first time he touched me, I invited more. He showed me things my younger sexual partners didn't know or wouldn't do. When I fell in love with him, it was giddy and all-in. I couldn't wait to get to work every day. The weekends seemed endless.

The signs, of course, were obvious. The fact that I didn't hear a word from him from Friday afternoon until Monday morning should've flashed warning lights. But he always had an excuse. He had to go to Santa Barbara to see his mom, or to LA to visit with his dad. There were other hints as well—at work, he was all business unless he and I were the only ones there. Then he'd kiss the back of my neck while I was filling molds. Sometimes he'd pull me into the back office for a quickie.

Maybe a month into our affair, he arrived wearing his wedding ring. He'd forgotten to take it off that morning.

"You're married?" I stuttered.

"I thought you knew," was his answer.

When I insisted I was most definitely unaware of that fact, he fed me a story about how he and his wife were talking divorce. Their relationship had cooled over the years, but their financial entanglements complicated things. I was the bright light in his days. She was the pain. I didn't believe it—not really. But I did accept it. And therein lies my complicity.

That strong moral sense I'd always laid claim to? Compromised. The hurt I felt at his dishonesty? Tucked away. The small hint of guilt I experienced over sleeping with another woman's husband vanished when he kissed me. Any notion of being used paled in comparison to being wanted.

He was married. But I was pretty—beautiful, he told me more than once. *He was married.* But I was desirable. *He was married.* But I wasn't the chubby girl, though I was still desperately seeking attention.

I don't know how long we might've continued seeing each other if his wife hadn't stopped by one day to bring him lunch. She was lovely. Gorgeous. Sweet.

She was also nine months pregnant.

She'd never been there before. I don't know if she got wind of things, or if it was a random visit. She gave no clue that she knew, but I watched her with Jim. She wasn't proprietary, but she swept across the floor and kissed him as any wife would, and the clear affection in her eyes told me all I needed to know.

When I quit, he didn't try to stop me.

I was stunned, and not just by him. The episode required deep introspection. Why was I willing to overlook his wife, but not the imminent arrival of his first child? Why was I okay with breaking up a marriage, but not a family? Looking back, I understand my limited perspective, and how that man took advantage of my relative innocence. He was at fault. But I could have said no.

Not long ago, my granddaughter left home. She was barely eighteen, and three months away from her high school graduation. Like me, she was abandoned by her parents. (She has lived with her paternal aunt since she was a toddler.) Like me, she has struggled with her weight and body image. And like me, she has been hungry for acceptance by her peers and boys.

She left a short goodbye note, got on a Greyhound, and traveled out of state to move in with a man seven years her elder. She promised she was okay, that there was no coercion. But her perspective is narrow, and some men are more than willing to capitalize on naivete.

I wish I would've confided this story to her. Instead, I'm confessing it to you, hoping it might save you the heartbreak I'm afraid my granddaughter will experience.

Take care of yourself. Believe in yourself. Love the person you are.

★ ★ ★ ★ ★

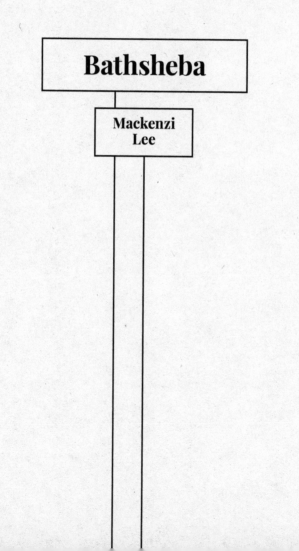

Bathsheba

Mackenzi
Lee

Leonard Cohen had it wrong: Bathsheba wasn't bathing on the roof.

In case you aren't familiar with that story from the Bible—or "Hallelujah," the song that references it—let's do a quick refresher. Or, rather, let me tell you my memory of it—how it was presented to me in Sunday school classrooms, over and over from the time I was twelve and just starting to be told that my existence as a woman in the world was really difficult for the men around me.

We begin with David, of David and Goliath fame. In a true rags-to-riches narrative, he was crowned king of Jerusalem, the chosen leader of one of God's chosen cities.

From the outside, it would appear that David was a pretty bitching king. But one day, he noticed a woman bathing on a rooftop near the palace. He was overcome by her beauty and asked his advisors or guards—or whoever was paid to hang out with the king—who the woman was. David learned that she was Bathsheba, the wife of one of his military commanders. It was lust at first sight, and when he summoned her to him, they began an affair. When she became pregnant with his child, he arranged for her husband to be killed in battle, so that he could marry her and save her from being stoned for adultery. Since God tends to frown upon both murder and adultery, it was the beginning of the end for David—the first stumble that became a fall from grace as his will and God's grew further and further apart.

As I remember it from church, the tale of David and Bathsheba was the story of a man who was tempted into sin by a woman. Bathsheba was a plot point in the tragic story of David's decline, with no narrative of her own. That's the version of the story that has crept into popular culture, and the one that I remember hearing while perched upon an uncomfortable folding chair in the chilly classrooms of the church of my youth. It was told to me from pulpits, sometimes in general assemblies addressed to the entire membership, sometimes to a small congregation by a leader I was taught to believe implicitly on all subjects, sometimes to a select group of young people. Once it was offered up by a male teacher to a room full of teenage women, alongside the moral that we "ought to be where we ought to be when we ought to be there." That was what he wanted us to take away from the story of David and Bathsheba the Harlot: we, as women, should not put ourselves in situations where we would inspire lust and sin in men. Bathsheba was bathing on the roof, a place where no woman should be naked unless she was asking for it. We should keep our necklines high and our heels low. Never drink too much, never lead men on, wear only one-piece bathing suits, so the reminder that we had bodies didn't inspire impure thoughts in the males around us. No one ever mentioned impure actions, though it wasn't hard to infer that those would be our fault, too.

We were Bathshebas.

We should not bathe on roofs.

But this is not the story at all.

The truth is that Bathsheba wasn't on the roof—David was. Bathsheba was indoors, likely in a communal bath house with other women, while David was *Rear Window*ing her from the palace rooftop.

The truth is that when David saw her, Bathsheba wasn't bathing at all. She was engaging in a holy purification ritual that orthodox Jews still practice. And not that it matters, but she was likely wearing clothes, because women at the time usually engaged in communal bathing while partially dressed. She had no idea she was being watched and sexualized while performing a sacred ritual.

The truth is that David didn't send an invitation for Bathsheba to come visit him, if it pleased her. He took her. He *took* her—that's how the Bible phrases it. He didn't write a love letter and then wait nervously by the phone for her to call. He sent soldiers to her house to remove her and bring her to him. She almost certainly did not grant her consent.

The truth is that, according to laws of the time, Bathsheba couldn't say no to her king if he demanded sex from her.

The truth is that, according to the laws, it wasn't rape unless the woman was a virgin, which David would have known Bathsheba likely wasn't, because she was married.

The truth is that David raped Bathsheba, and after the rape, when she became pregnant, David not only murdered her husband, but then also forced Bathsheba into a relationship with him. She was forced to marry and live with her rapist for the rest of his life.

The truth is that it was not an affair. It was not love.

Bathsheba was raped by a man in a position of power over her.

This was not the way the story was told to me.

I had to find out the truth on my own—totally by chance. It had never crossed my mind to seek out other versions of the Bible story I knew so well. Years after I left the church I grew up in, I was scrolling mindlessly through Facebook when an article passed through my timeline with a clickbait headline—"The Most Maligned Woman from the Bible." And because I'm baitable, I clicked it. Ten minutes later, it was like my whole world had shifted, everything I thought I knew recalibrated by the small details no one had ever mentioned in a story I had heard retold over and over again. The story of the woman that had been used my whole life as the ultimate example of how a good man could be led astray by a woman who did not keep her sexuality—or, really, existence—in check. The woman who had drifted through my thoughts when a man passed me sexually aggressive notes on the subway, then followed me home, as all the while I chastised myself for leading him on—for riding the subway late and alone, for wearing a dress without tights, for taking up space in his world. The woman who made me think, through my thick fear, that like Bathsheba, I deserved this. I had put myself here. I'd been bathing on the roof.

By the time I stumbled on the truth—hidden in my timeline as casually as a Buzzfeed quiz about which Chipotle menu item you are based on your zodiac sign—the damage had been done. I had already spent years feeling guilty for my own sexuality, trying to unravel the internalized misogyny born from hearing these stories of Bathsheba and women like her repeated long before I knew to question them, and carrying the responsibility of the behavior of the men around me on my shoulders. Never hearing the word *rape* or discussions of consent attached to these stories.

All I remembered was that if I bathed on a roof, whatever happened next would be my own fault.

Unsurprisingly, the world finds ways to continue to villainize Bathsheba and ignore her victimhood, the same as it continues to villainize survivors of sexual assault. Her name has become synonymous with *temptress*. She smolders from the cover of romance novels. In the most popular film of 1951, Susan Hayward swoons in Gregory Peck's arms beneath the title card, "The awe-inspiring story of the conquering Lion of Judah and the woman for whom he broke God's Own Commandments," followed by "The World's Greatest Love Story!" The paintings of her hanging in art museums around the world portray her breasts exposed, her naked body being presented to the viewer in a sprawl over the edge of a fountain. In the animated Bible stories children watch, David offers to marry her as a way to save her from death for adultery, her savior in love. As Leonard Cohen wrote in his iconic song, "Her beauty and the moonlight overthrew you," implying that what happened after he saw her bathing on the roof was out of David's control. He couldn't help it if he was overthrown.

I wish I could go back and retell Bathsheba's story to my younger self. This time, I would tell her Bathsheba was assaulted. She was taken. She was raped. I would not use soft words, the gentle words that were used in church sermons to imply but never speak its name.

I would give it a name.

Instead of a story about a man who was tempted by a woman, I would tell myself in no uncertain terms that it was not my responsibility to keep the men around me chaste. That I did not have to dress modestly to protect myself from predators, or to keep good young men from becoming predators. That I was not complicit in acts of sexual violence committed against me, no matter where I was bathing or what I was wearing or how many drinks I had or whether I was riding the subway alone.

I know it doesn't feel like any of this matters now, I would tell her. I know you think the world is kind. You don't think you will ever need to know words like *rape* and *assault*, or ever experience violence that you'll have to vocalize. From that Sunday school folding chair at twelve years old, you're sure you'll never be ogled, you'll never be forced somewhere, never be grabbed or touched against your will. Never have men yell at you from their cars. Never have partners who manipulate you into going further than you're comfortable, then blame you for tempting them into sin and saddle you with guilt you think is yours to carry for years.

But someday, when you retell your own life to yourself, I want you to know what to call these things. I want you to know it is not your responsibility to keep the men around you chaste. You don't have to dress modestly to protect yourself, you don't have to say yes when you mean no, you don't have to be polite to men who say things that make you uncomfortable, you don't have to smile. You are not a footnote in the story of a man's life. You are not a temptress, you are not a harlot, you are not responsible for the actions of the men around you—no matter where you are or what you're doing or what you are or aren't wearing while doing it.

That's what I wish I could tell myself: bathe wherever you damn well want.

★ ★ ★ ★ ★

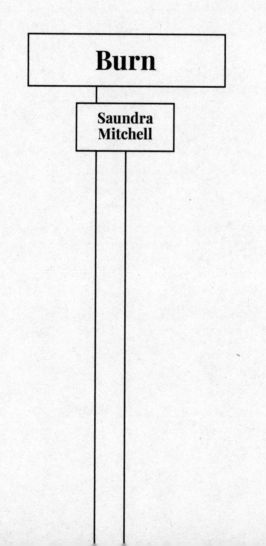

Burn

Saundra
Mitchell

Seventeen: on the steps of the student union, the middle of the night. A hand job I didn't want to give, to a guy I didn't like.

There were promises—bargains, really. I promised to be his girlfriend until midnight, the girl of his dreams for twenty-four hours. Not because it was magic or romantic or any of that—because he wouldn't stop *following* me, breathing on the back of my neck, appearing even when I slipped out of my classrooms and took the back halls to avoid him.

I don't remember his face, just the dusky heft of him in my hand. I may as well have been asleep, adorned in a glass coffin. Dead and animated at the same time, a warm, breathing masturbator because *he* needed, because *he* wanted. My feelings didn't matter. To him; to me.

And I know where it began. Back and back and back to:

Seven: in the brambles between a brick housing project and a cornfield, because Indiana always contrasts like that. With a stranger of a man who asked if I wanted to see something that would make me feel really good in the summer. His curls reminded me of my father's; his face seemed kind. Though my stomach rebelled, clenching against angry, uncertain waves, I bargained then, too. Aren't we supposed to respect our elders? So, I said, *I just want to see it.*

It was more than seeing, and I bargained on the way home. I would never tell, never, never, and it would go away and just be a dark seed in my heart, starved. But someone saw, and someone told, so twice that day, my flesh was not my own.

I think my mother cried; the police were tall, faceless shadows. The hospital was white, and more people touched me: *down there.* I was a filthy block of shame. *My fault*, I thought. I talked to a stranger, and bad things happen when you talk to strangers. Bad things. The worst thing. I should have known the difference between an elder and a stranger; shame on me. So much shame.

That's where I begin: a jumble of parts, a puppet off its strings. A body that belonged to everyone but me.

It belonged to the boy who lived next door to my parents' best friends, who pushed his tongue into my mouth and his hands beneath my T-shirt. (Twelve: there was nothing beneath my T-shirt; my body was still a vast and unshaped plain.) In my head, this is my first kiss, and I remember his name. It's a piece of poisoned apple, forever caught in my throat.

He pushed and pushed and pushed while my mother sat on the front porch, because she thought that we were cute, that she was letting us have a tiny, safe sliver of privacy. I didn't want it. How was it that the woman with eyes in the back of her head, who knew when I stole into the pantry for a forbidden oatmeal cream pie, *how* was it that she couldn't see what this boy was and what he wanted and what he would do?

I expected her to. I wanted her to. I wanted her to stay and fry green peppers and onions in the kitchen. To peek in and click her tongue and make sure we weren't *up to something*. Instead, she stayed outside, and talked to her friend. I heard her laugh, and died a little more. She didn't know.

And she didn't know thirteen: when my best friend slapped and pinched me until I let her call me John and agreed to learn her body under the gaze of a Duran Duran poster. That best friend, that girlfriend, never touched me, because she insisted: *she was not a lesbian* (!!!) and my shapelessness was still too female for her.

My gender swam back and forth, male and female, everything and nothing. I moved in those waters, easily. Wanting her and loving her was easy. But not the slaps. Not the punches. Not the bites and pinches and vicious twists, my flesh between her forefinger and thumb—her nails, long and sharp.

I took it; I thought I deserved it (Didn't I deserve it? Wasn't I bad? Wasn't I dirty? I was lucky she wanted to be my friend at all, considering my filth. Lucky, I thought, so lucky—hurt and bruised and lucky...).

My rescue was simply this: I chose a different high school, and then we weren't on the bus together anymore. My leaden legs stopped walking to her house. I drifted away from her passively, aloft on a little reed boat in a dark, dark sea.

Fourteen brings only enough shape to mock—the boy I thought was beautiful and brilliant and smart pricked me with an enchanted barb. It was so sharp, so cursed, that I still feel its sting sometimes, when I catch a glimpse of my body today. He said, carelessly, cleverly, that I was so flat, I was concave: a reverse treasure chest. The boy—no, man, because he was eighteen and should have been dating eighteen-year-old girls—who'd claimed me laughed.

That man dropped me into his bed. His waterbed, with Duran Duran on the radio. Like Rumpelstiltskin, he was the smart kind of vile. The bed took up most of the room; I drowned in its uneasy sea. During what I considered my first time, he wanted me to perform in ways he'd seen in pornography. In ways I'd never imagined.

What is yes when you can't say no? It's fourteen years old and trying to be sexy and clawing hands around (barely there) breasts to hide them because the room's not dark enough to hide in. Light pierces through the slats of the shades, and yes is feeling dirty again and used again and scrubbing everything away afterward with a towel hard from drying on a clothesline.

For all my books and dreams and desires, the ones that said no torment comes without rescue…no one saved me. They tried *not* to save me. So many people knew that this man bedded me and hit me; that he pulled out my hair and stuck his hands up my skirt in public. Even my parents knew: fourteen and eighteen, even if they didn't know the rest. That arithmetic always equals something wrong, but they all looked away. All God's children got their own problems, or so my grandmother would say.

I finally broke up with the Beast (ran away from him, hid from him) because he hit me and threatened me and put his hands on my throat on a military installation. The MP who found us said we were causing a disturbance. That we should stop.

And then he walked away. The police. The military *police*. Left me, red heat on my throat and terrified and humiliated. Left me to sew together tatters and escape without a Fairy Godmother at the ready. The Beast meant it when he tightened his hands on my throat—that he would kill me if I didn't shut up. And the military (!) police (!) told me that he would get away with it. No one would save me; I had to save myself.

The damsel in that dress had to jump from the window and land hard, all alone. That day, I fled and hid and lost all my friends, because *he* kept them, but at least I was free of him. Free of *that* particular dungeon. The Beast never turned into a prince; he'd never been one to begin with.

Fourteen and fourteen and fourteen—the old man at Union Station who had to stop to talk to me about the shape of my butt, and who offered me money for a "date."

(I was just there, exploring the new arcade with my friends; no, of course no, I already knew where tickets to Pleasure Island ended. But, "no, thank you," because I couldn't be rude, no no no.)

Fourteen, the man in the mall when I skipped school. He needed help finding his car. He needed it from me, the lost girl who was treating the bookstore like a library and hiding behind her backpack. He wasn't big, just bad; just a wolf who lied about a lost Lexus because he wanted me to come closer. I didn't; I saw his teeth at a distance. I recognized their flash.

Fourteen, the man who walked up to me at a park, in the dark, and insisted that I listen to his troubles, who wanted my comfort and encouragement. (I was naive enough to think that I was just the kind of person that people—men—wanted to talk to. Mirror Scheherazade, listening for a thousand nights instead of speaking.)

Sixteen was a little cleaner. I fell in love with a boy who said he loved me, too—he even shouted it over a lake, in the dark. His voice washed out in waves, and came back, and I believed the words.

Sometimes, I still hear those echoes. They strike my skin; they ring like bells at midnight.

But he went away, and in came dark suitors: the boy with the soft tongue, who tasted like cigarettes; the boy who could limbo lower than anyone I'd ever met and didn't want to introduce me to his friends; another girl who wanted me to transform her with my fingers, but hide my body in the shadows.

They wanted me to be a Nothing Cinderella. Transparent skin, a screen of a face, blank and ready for projection. Ears open to remember every single detail—he likes yellow cake with chocolate icing, and she eats pizza only if it's pepperoni and mushroom. A brain, a database, to catalog other people's desires, and no need to have any of my own.

That's why, at *seventeen*, it seemed reasonable to negotiate twenty-four hours, giving myself away from one midnight to the next. That boy on the steps, who followed me and demanded my time, his need was deep, and my no didn't matter. So, it made sense to say, "I'll be your girlfriend for twenty-four hours. I'll do what you want, anything you want, but it ends at midnight." It made sense to stuff down my feelings, and myself, and my revulsion, and my fear, and just let him have what he wanted—a hand job on the steps of the student union. It made sense to make myself into nothing.

After all, at thirteen, I was worth fifty dollars in a downtown mall. At twelve, I was good for wet and messy desperation behind a shed. At seven, I said I only wanted to see it, but he insisted on so much more.

It all threaded together, a disaster of a ball gown. It wound black ribbons around my throat and cinched tight beneath my disappointing breasts. A foot pressed into my back to tighten the stays, to take away my breath—I didn't need to breathe. I didn't need to speak. All I needed were skirts that floated like gauze and shimmered like gossamer and lifted with the lightness of a feather.

But midnight struck. Hard. And something shattered. The glass slippers, my porcelain shell, the capsule that kept my blood from flowing. There, on the steps of the student union, I broke, and I realized:

I belong to myself.

I am my own. I don't have to be here.

I wasn't a princess. No sugar and spice—I was made of fury and flame. I rose up, a phoenix, and I became something different.

Something that said *no*, and *hell no*, and didn't care about being polite to all the wolves and beasts.

Some*one* who no longer secretly believed that I had deserved it, that I had earned those punches and slaps and grasping, gripping fingers.

Someone who realized that some people just *take*. They steal. They lie; they devour. No one should be taken for a trick when they're just trying to buy a book or feed another quarter into a video game.

Someone who realized that there's never something that feels good in the summer, never a missing puppy, never a lost car in the mall parking lot. That he won't die if he doesn't get it; that the boy who just won't give up isn't a prince.

He's a predator.

I'd like to say that what came after seventeen was perfection. That it was simple and easy and sunlight scoured away all the darkness. No.

After seventeen was *better*, but it's still life. The world is the world, and there are still moments when the monsters creep into view. But I'm not, *we're* not, combing our hair in towers anymore. Anger is kindling, and we feed it when we press it down deep. We put that fire under pressure, again and again, trying to hide from it.

We build a phoenix with every emotion we swallow, with every touch taken from us, from every smile forced. We burn and we burn and we burn from the inside, until there's nothing holding us back.

We explode.

I exploded. When a friend told me that another Beast spiked her punch and stole everything under her clothes, I exploded. I threw orange juice in his face in the middle of the cafeteria. I called him a rapist and dared him to say anything back.

I started writing, my flames cauterizing the page with anger and emotion and all those *NO*s I'd swallowed. My voice rose up, out loud, in script. On protest boards and letters to the editor. In literary magazines and little bitty films. In novels. In essays. In this book.

The world trembles before angry women, because angry women no longer tremble. We don't care if someone thinks we should smile; we strike back. Sometimes we strike first. The look on the face of the first man I told, "Touch me and you'll pull back a stump," is the sweetest fuel. It burns clean and hot; it cleanses. It renews.

I am a phoenix. And I am not alone.

There are phoenixes everywhere. If you look, you can see them blazing on the horizon. It's not just you—it's her too, it's him too, it's them too, and you can find your way by their light.

There's fear and anger and fury in those conflagrations. There are words people want to soften, but nothing softens fire. Fire *is*, we *are*, and if you are too, come burn with us. Even if you're afraid, if you think you tend only a spark, come closer.

Together, we burn and blaze; together, we swallow the shadows and leave no room for beasts or bastards. We illuminate the night and we drive them out. We leave their ashes in our wake.

I'm not a princess. I'm a free Saundra, and I belong to no one but myself. You are a free creature, and you belong to no one but yourself. Your *heart* matters. Your *anger* matters. Your *NO* matters.

So, come on. Come with me.

Let's burn this mother down.

★ ★ ★ ★ ★

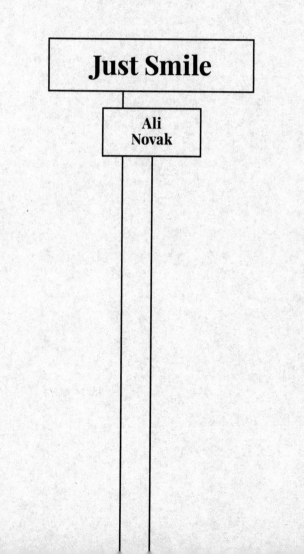

Just Smile

Ali
Novak

It was supposed to be the perfect summer job. All I had to do was stock the beverage cart, sell a few beers and soak up the sun. At least, that's how my friend Dave convinced me to apply for the position. He was a waiter at South Valley, a private country club in our small town, and he'd recently heard about an opening on the bar team.

"You don't even have to drive around the course like a regular cart girl," he'd told me. "There's a pavilion between holes five and thirteen. You park underneath it and wait for the golfers to come to you."

"Why?" I remember asking. At the time, I had only a vague idea of what a standard cart girl's job entailed. I'd never once stepped foot on a golf course, and my knowledge of the sport was limited to the following: Phil Mickelson was a famous golfer, holes-in-one were rare, and players used an assortment of clubs to whack a tiny white ball into a sequence of holes.

But I was curious. Wasn't the whole point of having a refrigerator on wheels…to be mobile? To appear on the crest of a grassy hill like a ministering angel so as to quench the thirst of dehydrated golfers on a too-hot day? Clearly, I'd romanticized the job in my head, but after three years of smelling like chlorine and watching lap swimmers, I was over lifeguarding.

"I'm not entirely sure. Possibly because the beverage cart is ancient? It sounds like a gigantic metal beast that's falling apart one bolt at a time. Maybe the members don't want the noise disrupting their shots? Most are pretty serious about their game." He shrugged, then added, "Trust me. Not driving around is a good thing. You'll have a ton of downtime to read or write or whatever. Think about it, Ali. How awesome would it be if we worked together?"

Being able to read on the job was tempting, but… "I don't have any experience in the service industry," I pointed out. As a lifeguard, I'd held a position of authority, enforcing pool rules with the blow of a whistle and a stern voice. *The customer is always right* was a foreign concept to me.

Dave waved off my concerns. "Don't worry. You're exactly what they're looking for. They'll hire you on the spot."

And he was right.

The day of my interview, my stomach was an empty pit of nerves and dread. How could I apply three years of lifeguarding and my babysitting experience to a bartending position? I doubted my ability to backboard a swimmer with a possible spinal injury was necessary, or that my hide-and-seek expertise would be appreciated. But Rob, the bar manager, didn't care about my work history. After introducing himself, he looked me up and down and asked if I'd be free to start training the next day.

This threw me for a loop. "Yes, I'm available, but…what about the interview?"

A grin stretched across Rob's face. "We don't need to bother with formalities. When you've been in the business as long as I have, you know how to spot a good cart girl. And let me tell you, Ali—I have a feeling that you'll be perfect."

I frowned, trying to figure out what quality I possessed that Rob had picked up on during the two minutes he'd known me. The truth was, he—and Dave, for that matter—understood something important I hadn't grasped at the time: my qualifications and character had zero effect on whether or not I got the job, but my appearance did. This was all about my body, and it wasn't until I started working at South Valley that I realized how naive I'd been.

Becca, the head cart girl, scanned my outfit and shook her head when I showed up for my first day of work. "You're going to need to change if you want to earn good tips."

"But this is what Rob told me to wear," I replied, confused yet again. He'd gone over my uniform after hiring me—khaki shorts or a skirt that reached past my fingertips, a blue polo, and tennis shoes to protect my feet.

"He's required to tell you the official uniform because he's the bar manager, but none of us cart girls actually wear it. Get some khaki short shorts. Your polo is okay, but tighter is better, and bright blues like aqua and turquoise attract more attention. As for your bra—"

"What's wrong with my *bra*?"

"Nothing, technically. You've got great boobs, but believe me—a push-up bra never hurts."

Cheeks flushing, I asked, "We won't get in trouble?" My

lifeguarding background had ingrained in me a respect for rules, and breaking them my first day on the job seemed ludicrous.

"I've been working here for two years and nobody's said a word to me about it. The members like to see a little skin. Well, the guys do, anyway. Most of the wives are stuck-up and don't tip regardless of what you're wearing, so don't worry about them."

Oh, God. What had I gotten myself into?

The apprehension must have been clear on my face, because Becca smiled. "Don't be nervous. Majority of the members here are super nice and well behaved, I promise. It's nothing like working on a public course."

"What do you mean?"

"Well, I used to be a cart girl down at Myrtle Beach. All the golfers there are on vacation. They want to have a good time, blow off steam, and they know they'll never see the cart girl again, so that makes them brazen. I've had plenty of guys slip me their hotel key card and tell me to visit them once I finish my shift. I've been patted and squeezed like an animal at a petting zoo, and one time, a guy offered me a hundred-dollar bill to take off my top."

Becca answered my question with an air of nonchalance that made me wonder: Was she just that thick-skinned, or did she wear her indifference like armor?

Despite her horror stories, Becca's promise about the members of South Valley being well behaved held true for the most part. I quickly made friends with a plethora of regulars: there was D.J. Villager, an investment banker who always tipped me a Jackson and reminded me of a washed-up rock star; Mr. Kowalski, a drunk so loud you could hear him coming from two holes away, who always ordered a Captain and Coke, hold the Coke; and Mr. Deeker, a retiree who brought me coffee every Sunday morning and loved talking about his grandkids.

There was only one regular at South Valley who made me feel uncomfortable. His name was Mr. Lannester, but all the cart girls called him Mr. Handsy behind his back. He was a huge guy with broad shoulders and a protruding belly, so if he managed to pull you into a side hug, his favorite move, there was no escape—he'd hold you against his sweat-soaked shirt until he was done rubbing you down like some kind of perverse, unwanted massage therapist. As a result, I had to be on my toes around Mr. Lannester, constantly dancing away from his outstretched arm. He reminded me of a claw from a toy crane game, always reaching, reaching, reaching. Unfortunately for all of us cart girls, he scored his prize far more often than kids at an arcade. To add to the torture, Mr. Lannester regularly golfed with his son, Jay, who was the same age as me. I didn't mind Jay. Unlike his father, he was polite and kept his hands to himself. The problem was, after his routine fondling session, Mr. Lannester made a habit of trying to get Jay and me to date. He loved talking about why his son was a better option for me than my current boyfriend, how we'd make a handsome couple, and that I'd be a perfect addition to the family. All after groping my butt.

I quickly learned the best way to deal with unpleasant situations was to nod my head and smile. After all, I was all alone on the golf course. None of my coworkers were there to help me fend off unwanted attention. And although it wasn't part of my job description, members expected me to play the part of bubbly, flirty cart girl. If I didn't participate in their game, I didn't earn the extra cash I needed for college. So, if someone told a dirty joke? I grinned like I'd never heard a better punchline. Someone touched me? I beamed as if my skin wasn't crawling. I became an actress who was perpetually happy and impervious to the inappropriate, and despite these unwanted encounters, I stayed at South Valley because the money was good. But everyone has a tipping point. No one can balance on the edge forever.

For me, that moment came during my third summer working as a cart girl. By then I thought I'd heard it all, every vulgar come-on and cliché pickup line under the sun. I even thought I'd grown thicker skin as a result.

I had never been more wrong in my life.

On the last weekend of every month, South Valley rented out its course to local businesses interested in hosting charity outings. That meant the majority of golfers I served were strangers or, as Becca liked to call them, wild cards. You never knew if the guests would be a professional group of businessmen or a crowd of partiers.

It was during one of these events when it happened. Since the weather was terrible—gray, cold, and misting—the beer-selling business was slow, and I had my nose buried in a book.

"Hey there, honey."

I startled in my seat to discover a foursome parked in front of me. "Oh, hi. I'm sorry. I didn't hear you drive up."

The men laughed. They were young, late twenties or early thirties. Closest to me was a heavyset man in a TaylorMade visor with a cigar between his lips. His partner, who bared his teeth at me in what was probably meant to be a charming smile, wore sunglasses, despite the overcast sky. The final two men appeared to be twins and were sporting tie-dye pants from Loudmouth—a sportswear brand known for colorful, in-your-face apparel that was popular with golfers.

"Must be a good book," said TaylorMade. "Whatcha reading?"

"A Game of Thrones." I shut the paperback, stood, and pulled out the standard opener I liked to use on strangers: "So, how's everyone playing?"

My question was ignored. *"Game of Thrones,* huh? That's a big book for such a little lady. You strike me as more of a romance girl."

Wow, okay. I tucked a strand of hair behind my ear, mentally preparing myself for what would in all probability be an annoying encounter. "Actually, I read a bit of everything."

"How about *Fifty Shades of Grey?"* Sunglasses asked, flashing me another unnerving grin. His friends hooted with laughter.

It was time to change the subject. "What can I get you gentlemen to drink?"

TaylorMade slung an arm around my shoulder. "You're not getting off the hook that easily, Blondie. We want to hear your thoughts on the book."

"Sorry, I haven't read that one," I lied. No way was I discussing erotica with these men.

"Cindy *loves* those books. Made her want to try all this kinky shit in the bedroom," Twin Number One said. "It was awesome."

"Yeah?" his brother replied. "Like what?"

"One time she let me handcuff her to the bed, and then I surprised her with some nipple clamps."

"How'd she like it?"

"Howled like a banshee. I've never cummed so fast in my life."

There was another round of wild laughter.

TaylorMade squeezed me tighter against his side. "I bet Blondie here would look great in nipple clamps. What do you think, boys?"

Everyone turned their attention to me. My stomach churned. How was it possible to feel both exposed and insignificant at the same time? *Just smile,* I remember telling myself. *Smile, and this will all be over soon.* The next five minutes passed in a blur, my mind and body on autopilot as I made four vodka lemonades and rang the men up. Once they were gone, I locked myself in the tiny restroom attached to the pavilion and cried.

I never told anyone what happened to me that day on the golf course. Instead, I pushed the memory deep down. I thought the best way to heal was to move on. If I spoke up, I'd have to relive the experience over again. On top of that, I was worried what people would think of me. After all, I was the one who chose to work at South Valley. I was the one who decided to wear short shorts, a tight top, and a push-up bra to make better tips. *Besides,* I told myself. *The things those men said? They're just words.*

But words have power, and although I wasn't physically harmed, the emotional trauma those men inflicted affected me for years. I developed anxiety, and my self-confidence dropped so low I started wearing minimizer bras to hide the size of my chest.

When I first heard of the #MeToo movement, I thought my story didn't matter. No one sexually assaulted me, I never reported the incident, and it happened so long ago. Sharing my story might trivialize the experience of individuals who suffered through nightmares compared to me. But as more survivors came forward, as I read accounts both similar and vastly different to my own, I realized that way of thinking was part of the problem.

I'm telling my story now to make a change, because even though words have the power to tear you down and strip you of your strength, they also have the ability to inspire, uplift, and evoke change. I'm telling my story now so a traumatizing experience can transform into a positive action I hope will protect other people. I'm telling my story now so another scared girl won't be forced to just smile.

★ ★ ★ ★ ★

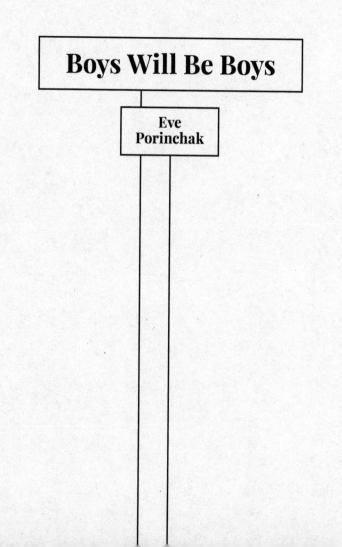

Boys Will Be Boys

Eve Porinchak

Miss Galen shook her head with a smirk. "Oh no, honey," she said. "You are way too pretty to become a doctor or psychologist. How about you become a model? Then you can *marry* a doctor or psychologist, okay?"

Miss Galen was our classroom assistant. Late in our sixth-grade year, we created time capsules to be revisited ten years later. When she asked what I would become when I grew up, I said I wanted to help people, especially little kids. "I'm planning to become a doctor or child psychologist."

Unsatisfied with my response, Miss Galen wrote down her own answer for me and stuffed it into my time capsule. I returned to my desk, defeated, but not entirely surprised. It was not the first time I was judged based on my looks—nor would it be my last.

Rewind to six months earlier in the year, when it became apparent to me that boys were treated differently than girls. Our K–6 elementary school was on a year-round schedule; we attended school for three months, with three weeks off, and then repeated. We were divided up into cycles, supposedly based on intelligence—no joke. We had to take IQ tests and everything. I was part of Cycle C, the cream of the intelligence crop. It was no secret that the rest of the school labeled the kids in Cycle C as homely, dorky misfits who scored high on tests but failed in popularity. But I always had a fire inside me and didn't believe in fitting into one category. Why couldn't I be smart *and* cool?

My family had moved from the rural woods of Maryland to super-hip Southern California during the summer before fifth grade. Still, I had an ultracool mother who had sported Beatnik chic in 1960s London. And I had a sister two years older who lived and breathed cutting-edge fashion. Therefore, I had the luxury of a direct pipeline to the hookup on soon-to-be-trending ensembles. Although we didn't have the finances to support my sister's fashion habits, she made do. She and her progressive eighth-grade friends scoured thrift stores, refurbished my mom's vintage velvet blazers, and slipped on her decades-old skinny pegged pants.

Eventually, my sister and her girlfriends discovered leg warmers. Hardly necessary in inland Southern California—the temperature dropped to its chilliest at around seventy degrees—but they didn't care. They were so fashion forward! One day, my mom noticed me coveting my sister's threads. She immediately went out and bought me my very own purple leg warmers with silver strands weaved through them. To this day, I've never been so excited about a gift. She had also purchased the perfect outfit to pair with the leg warmers—

a bulky gray sweater dress, not too tight, not too short. In fact, it hung down to my knees, where it met the tops of the leg warmers. Still, I wasn't into showing skin, so we picked up some sparkly silver tights to wear under the dress. Yeah, I know, I'm sweating just remembering it.

Before my best friend CJ and I made the short walk to school on the day I was to debut my new outfit, I dug through my mom's makeup drawer. There I discovered the plastic case of green glitter CoverGirl eye shadow that I had dreamed of wearing someday. It was perfect! Because, really, what complements a purple-and-silver getup more than half-moons of sparkling green? I swiped a thick line of powder onto each eyelid, then inspected myself in the mirror.

I'd never seen my face with makeup before, and I immediately regretted my decision to put it on. It felt wrong, like I was doing something I wasn't ready for. And there was too strong a resemblance to the young hooker I had seen in that late-night rated-R movie CJ and I had just watched. A month or so prior, I had developed seemingly overnight. Although I was only eleven, almost twelve, I grew breasts, hips, and height. At five feet five inches tall and wearing an obviously ill-fitting, lumpy bra, I looked more like an older sister than a friend next to my peers. I was not ready for breasts and menstrual cramps and hair on my legs, but there it was—womanhood.

Wearing makeup, at least, was something I could control. I scrubbed it off.

The minute we arrived at Royal Elementary School, something was different. Boys stared at me. Teachers were whispering. I had never really stood out or flashed any kind of fineness before that day. But suddenly, I felt noticeable. And not in a good way. Boys whistled at me. They asked if I was "easy." I had no clue what that meant—until they chased me at recess and grabbed my butt. It was like, in a blink, our juvenile dynamic had flipped upside down. We weren't playing innocent games of tag anymore. This felt predatory and scary. My day of coming out as smart *and* cool was a disaster.

At lunchtime, my teacher pulled me aside and announced that the principal wanted to see me in his office. Now, mind you, I was a good kid—the best kind of kid. Getting sent to the principal's office was a huge deal. Having always been a rule follower with an outrageously high respect for authority figures, I could not have imagined a worse punishment.

Then I had an epiphany. Maybe *I* wasn't in trouble. Maybe the principal was calling me in to let me know that the *boys* were in trouble for treating me like an object, and he was making *them* apologize to *me* for acting so monstrous.

So I walked with confidence toward Principal Port's office. He closed the door behind me. I sat. He stared. He looked me up and down.

"Does your, uh, mother know you're dressed this way?" he asked.

The question confused me. "My mother bought me this outfit, sir."

"Well, uh," he said. "We've had some complaints."

"Complaints? What kind of complaints?"

He took a deep breath. "Well, people have said that you, uh… you are wearing, well, something an older girl might wear."

"Like my sister in eighth grade?"

"Exactly."

"Is that against the rules?"

"Yes. Well, no. It's just. Well, you look older…"

"Yeah, I know. I can't help that."

Principal Port became flustered at that point. His face grew red. "You need to go home and change!"

"Change? My clothes?"

"Yes."

I remember feeling horrified at the thought of walking home, changing clothes, then returning to my classroom in a completely different outfit. What would my classmates think?

"I could, I guess." Still, I could not understand what I had done wrong. So I asked, "I'm curious, sir. Have I broken any school rules? Did I violate the dress code in any way?"

"Yes. I mean no. But, well, boys are going to think... They are, well, they want to..."

It was silent then. Principal Port did not need to continue. I knew exactly what he meant. Although my outfit was not revealing in any way, and did not break school rules, the sight of me, a twelve-year-old child in a woman's body, made people uncomfortable. Made my classmates uncomfortable. Made *him* feel uncomfortable. The sweater dress, the flashy leg warmers, the confidence I radiated, all somehow became sexualized.

I stormed off to my classroom, grabbed my backpack, and walked home. It's not that I was acting like a defiant smartass toward Principal Port on purpose. I just wanted straight answers. Even at age twelve, I felt in my bones this scenario was unfair. My parents had instilled a firm sense of justice in my sister and me since birth. We had very few rules in our household. In fact, we had four: Don't lie. Don't cheat. Don't steal. And always, *always* speak up and stand up for what is right and just.

I'd never broken a rule, or rebelled, or failed to do anything a grown-up had ever asked me to do. But that day, I walked home. I did not change my clothes. And I did not return to school. I waited for my supercool, fashion-forward mom to come home from a long day working her hospital shift. Our family processed my feelings of anger at the inequity of how the situation was handled. And then we laughed. "Potato sack ensembles for you from now on!" they would say while I got dressed in the mornings.

From that point on, being a sixth-grader with breasts and hips pretty much doomed me to endless harassment simply for being larger and curvier than my classmates. This is where the story gets worse. Like I said, I was enrolled in a year-round school system. That meant we had to walk to school, play outside at recess, endure physical education (usually dodgeball, which was really just a vehicle of torture meant to amuse our teachers), and then walk home in ninety-plus-degree heat for a month or so.

That June, the girl version of boys' surfer shorts had debuted. Dolfin shorts were light and breezy, dried quickly, and sported elastic waistbands that were just downright comfortable. They featured every color, stripe combo, and pattern one could imagine. Perfectly acceptable in our school, Dolfin shorts fit into the dress code and, quite honestly, I cannot remember a single girl who didn't wear them.

As the days grew sweltering, the Dolfin shorts came out. The walk from school to my home was roughly half a mile through a safe suburban neighborhood. My best friend CJ and I walked to and from school together most days. Occasionally, CJ had to leave school early for chiropractic appointments to treat her scoliosis. On those days, I walked home alone.

Two very popular boys—let's call them Rylan and Manny—began following me home when CJ wasn't around. They were taller and beefier than the other boys in our grade. These were not boys who talked to me at school. They ran in a different crowd. When I felt them following me, I'd walk faster, and for a while, I made it home safely. Then they started chasing me at full speed until I reached my house and locked myself inside. I couldn't imagine what they wanted with me. After several weeks, they found shortcuts, ways to spring out at me from behind cars and such while I walked my usual route home. Soon, their motive became apparent.

A couple times, they moved close enough to grab me from behind and pull at the elastic waistband of my shorts. Once, however, things got out of hand. I was four houses away from mine, with no stalkers in sight. I decided to take a detour to visit a friend who went to a different school. As I climbed up the Rileys' driveway, I heard the familiar feet clomping toward me. Rylan and Manny grabbed me from behind and shoved me down an alley, where a two-foot white-brick wall separated two houses. There were no sounds. Manny sat down on the wall, yanked me onto his lap, and leaned backward, pinning me against his stomach. When I say these two boys were "beefier" than others, I should make note that Manny was *literally* a giant—the result of some congenital pituitary gland hormone dysfunction. Rylan stood in front of us and tugged at my lime-green–and–white-striped Dolfin shorts. I kicked and screamed, and I remember thinking how easily my stretchy shorts could be taken off.

Soon those shorts were draped around my ankles. The memory that stands out the most for me is their laughter. Whooping, hollering laughter. The time frame may have been seconds, or minutes. I have no idea. It felt like hours. I was unsure if my underwear had been dragged down with my shorts. But as I kicked and squirmed, I felt their skin against mine in parts of my body that had never been touched before.

Nausea. I remember waves of nausea and my stomach cramping. I had no idea what was coming, or what was even possible. It's strange to have a primal fear of the absolute un-known. I had never touched or been touched by a boy. And I did not completely understand the mechanics of sex. I hadn't really paid attention to sex education in fifth grade because CJ and I were giggling uncontrollably, and it kind of grossed me out. So, it's not as if I thought, "Now I am going to be raped." Still, the intense fear tore through my body. All I knew was that I needed to get away as quickly as I could, and I had lost all sense of safety. Four houses away from my home.

When we heard a man's voice call out, "What's going on down there?" the two boys fled. I have no idea which neighbor it was. I'm sure he retreated back to his tract house, wanting nothing to do with the aftermath of an attack on a young girl.

I pulled my shorts up. I grabbed my backpack. And I ran home. I made a conscious decision not to tell my parents about the incident. First, I wanted to forget about it and move on. I was not "harmed" physically, so I figured all was well. Second, my family is fiercely protective. I can guarantee that if I'd told them, Rylan and Manny would have ended up (at best) hospitalized, or (at worst) dead. In fact, I never told anybody about what Manny and Rylan had done. Until...

One day, I noticed a brand-new recess monitor in the schoolyard. I liked her immediately. She smiled between pink doughy cheeks. She stopped kids swinging around the monkey bars from performing deadly cherry drops (something I had repeatedly warned could cause neck injury and subsequent paralysis). She punished girls who shouted nasty names like "bra stuffer" and "pig" at other girls. She seemed like an ally.

I was shocked to discover she was Manny's mother.

Over time I reasoned that since this kid's mother was a good person, maybe she could stop him from becoming a bad one. I gathered the courage to approach Manny's mother and describe exactly what he and Rylan had done to me. I expected a giant gasp, followed by a giant ass-whooping of

Manny in front of the entire school. (That's what parents did in the 1980s. Don't judge.) Instead, Manny's cherubic mother stood there blinking at me. Finally, she said, "Are you Eve?"

"Yes." I nodded. "I'm Eve. You've heard of me?"

"Yeah." She paused. "I heard you were a *whore*."

When I ran straight to Principal Port to report what Manny and Rylan had done and what Manny's mother called me, he replied with a short speech—I'm paraphrasing here—"Well, what do you expect to happen if you look like that and dress the way you do?"

Years later I ran into Manny at a party. Clearly, the fight portion of the fight-or-flight response kicked into gear, because I marched right up to him and blasted him in front of everybody. He had no clue what I was talking about. He honestly did not remember chasing or attacking me. He shrugged and said something like, "We did that stuff all the time. We didn't hurt anybody. We were just having fun."

Ah, the old *boys will be boys* defense. To quote the film *Thelma and Louise*, "In the future, when a woman's crying like that, she isn't having any fun."

It's not that Manny didn't remember being a perpetrator. He just didn't remember assaulting me specifically. I had expected him to respond one of two ways. He could have lied and said it never happened, or he could have apologized.

He did neither. His response was worse. He excused and normalized his behavior.

Ironically, those events of my sixth-grade year worked in my favor. Some kind of fireball of justice exploded in my belly. From that year forward, I grew fiercely protective of anybody who was judged based on their looks. Any uninvited gropes or attacks aimed at me or my friends ended poorly for the perpetrators. And despite Miss Galen's lack of confidence in me, Principal Port's overt sexism, Rylan and Manny's vile behavior, and the recess monitor's disgraceful response to my story—*or perhaps because of them*—I developed into an independent, resilient teenager, and then a woman. My goal in life became twofold: prove my antagonists wrong, and never let somebody else define what I am. Somehow, I harnessed the negative energy spewed from those people to fuel my drive, fearlessness, and subsequent success.

A former sixth-grade classmate recently posted an old photo of our entire Cycle C class on social media. That grainy photo documented a pivotal moment in my life. In the picture, I am wearing a white polo shirt, with the collar propped up, and my lime-green–and–white-striped Dolfin shorts. In the right margin, my quote says, *"When I grow up I'd like to be a fashion model and marry a doctor!"*

Joke's on you, Miss Galen. When the sixth-grade time capsule arrived at my house exactly ten years later, I had just graduated from UCLA with a degree in psychology. Afterward, I went to medical school.

Manny currently teaches high school. He also coaches girls' sports. He and Rylan are both fathers—to young daughters. I constantly wonder if they ever see me when they look at their young girls, and how they would react if two schoolmates stalked, then attacked their children. Do they become gripped with anxiety every time they see pubescent boys around their daughters? I secretly hope they do.

★ ★ ★ ★ ★

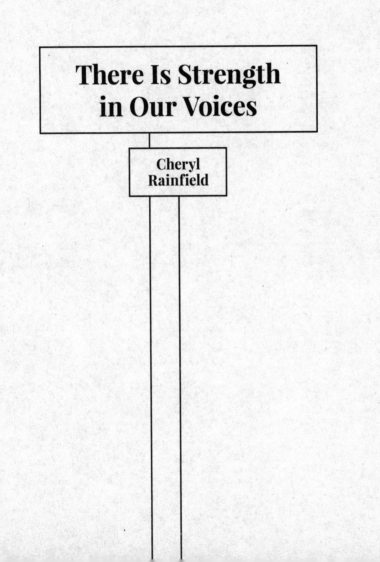

There Is Strength
in Our Voices

Cheryl
Rainfield

I was taught as a child that I had to endure rape, abuse, and torture, that I had to keep quiet about it, and that it was my fault. My parents and extended family were part of intergenerational, interconnected cults, and rape, torture, and mind control were daily/nightly experiences used to control me and the other children. My abusers taught me that any reaction to the trauma was an overreaction, that all I deserved was abuse and that no one would ever believe me if I talked.

It took me years and years to overcome that. But even though I blamed myself, I knew deep down that what my abusers were doing was wrong.

I felt such overpowering, intense emotional pain while being raped and tortured, and seeing others be raped and tortured. There was no way I could watch the other kids suffer and cry out and not realize that what was being done to them was wrong. I couldn't understand how my abusers could hurt others and not feel their pain when it was so obvious on every level. How they could be immune to it or, worse, enjoy it. I vowed to never be like my abusers, to never hurt others and cause such intense pain.

So many times, I wanted to die. I never wanted anyone else to feel as badly as I felt, to feel so bad they didn't want to live, so I repeatedly tried to stop my abusers from hurting others, even though it meant they would hurt me more. The abuse and torture were so traumatic that I had to dissociate—to split off parts of myself—and suppress the memories of abuse while they were happening in order to survive.

My parents and other cult members not only raped and tortured me and the other children, but they also sold our bodies to other abusers (child prostitution); took photos and films of the rape and torture and sold those (child pornography); and made derogatory and lewd comments about our bodies. But you wouldn't know just by looking at my parents what they were doing in secret. They and the other cult members were great at social masks—if you didn't look beneath the veneer or didn't have highly attuned gut reactions to people. My parents didn't look like monsters; they looked like a normal, middle-class, working couple. They knew the (mostly) appropriate things to say, though they had no warmth. They both went to church every Sunday; my father taught Sunday school, my mother sang in the choir. My mother baked cookies for school bake sales and made crafts for the church bazaar. They sent me to local schools where at least one cult member volunteered or was on staff to keep tabs on me and the other victims. They demanded to know where I was at all times and to come home promptly after school, which just looked like overprotective parenting to most. They kept me isolated, only interacting with other families or people who were part of the cults, rarely ever going anywhere except school, home, and to visit other cult members. The only TV I could watch was *Sesame Street*, *Mr. Rogers' Neighborhood*, and *Mr. Dressup*, even when I was far too old for those shows. I did not have access to popular media or music, and I didn't even know how to use the subway until after I ran away. And they taught me to force a smile even when I was scared, sad, or in pain.

If you looked closely at me, though, I showed many signs of abuse. I was highly introverted and shy, did not willingly join in group activities, and did not have friends. I rarely spoke, and when I did, it was either too fast or too quiet for people to hear me. I had very low self-esteem, low self-confidence, and I blamed myself, criticized myself, and hated myself. I constantly apologized, and I was bullied at school. I jumped at touch and loud sounds; walked with my head hanging down, shoulders hunched, and my arms crossed over my body; in hallways or crowds I tightly twisted and turned my body so that no one would bump into or touch me; and for a few years, I walked facing the wall in school. I also started cutting after abuse memories resurfaced at age thirteen, and tried to kill myself.

I was terrified to speak; my abusers paired the rape and abuse with death threats, physical and psychological torture, and mind control. But I desperately needed safety and an end to the rape and torture, so I tried to tell without actually speaking—through my art, my writing, and the trauma I showed in my reactions. At school I drew pictures that hinted at what I was surviving, such as being tied to and tortured on an altar, and I wrote stories of animals and people being hunted. I didn't have safety, love, or anything remotely resembling safe touch, except a few teachers over the years. But books (and my empathy and imagination) told me that that was possible, and when I couldn't believe or hope for that, other parts of me did. I desperately hoped that someone would see what was happening and save me.

Finally, one day when I was in grade seven or eight, a teacher heard me through a story I wrote in class about a girl who was sexually abused. She asked me to stay after school, and then tried to get me to talk about what I'd written. I was so terrified I couldn't answer her questions—couldn't say anything at all—so she called in the police and the Children's Aid Society (the equivalent to Child Protective Services in the United States). I was too terrified to speak to the detective or social worker—I was still being abused and was living with my abusers, who threatened to kill me if I told—but I was able to write about my great-uncle who raped me but did not live with me. That and my obvious terror and trauma convinced the agency to put me into therapy (and my family into family therapy), and I got a little closer to safety. But because I was too terrified to speak, because my abuser parents and extended family were so good at social masks, and because the professionals involved didn't understand cult abuse or investigate my family, the rape, torture, and mind control continued, and actually increased because I'd told.

I kept working on remembering, healing, and trying to get safe.

Eventually, I was able to remember enough to know that I had to run away to get safe. I knew I couldn't survive on the street—I was so deeply vulnerable—so a few weeks after I turned seventeen, I ran away to a shelter. Each time I ran away, my abusers found me and abused me again. Because I'd suppressed so much of the abuse and split so much of myself to survive using dissociation and DID, sometimes I still trusted people who were part of the abuse because I didn't remember their involvement. I had to keep working on remembering what had happened and who had abused me, talking to a therapist who believed and supported me, and running away many times over many years before I was able to completely escape.

I had to be the one to save myself. And I had to keep filling my soul with messages that were opposite to the ones my abusers were telling me. I created a deck of affirmation cards because I found it easier to give positive messages to others than to myself. I wrote positive messages that I put on my walls and repeated them often to counteract all the self-hate I'd been taught, and I still do this. I realized that I had to love myself—*really* love myself, that I did not deserve to be hurt, not ever—not even by myself, and that I am lovable and loved, all of which is true of each of us. I remind my readers of that often. Those messages, along with therapy, helped me to stop self-harming.

Books—both fiction and nonfiction—were a big part of my finding new, positive messages and learning that I wasn't to blame and that I wasn't alone. I carried *The Courage to Heal*— a powerful book on healing for sexual abuse survivors—with me everywhere in high school, showing pages to people when I didn't have the words to explain the effects of the abuse. I devoured *Homecoming* by Cynthia Voigt, *Blubber* by Judy Blume, *Girl of the Limberlost* by Gene Stratton-Porter, and so many other books about strong girls overcoming trauma, abuse, bullying, pain, and oppression.

I couldn't find books that showed me characters surviving exactly what I had, or lesbians who were happy in relationships, which is part of why I write what I do. I write the books I needed as a teen and couldn't find. But the books I read still helped me. As a child, I didn't have the words to say that I was queer—and I didn't have any examples of queerness or a way to know that I wasn't alone, so I always said I would never marry (lesbians and gay men weren't legally allowed to marry then). Then, when I was sixteen, I got involved with my first partner. I'm grateful I was able to find some queer music, books, and community to turn to as a teen.

I didn't stop with books; I subscribed to survivor newsletters and sent in artwork, poetry, and the occasional article. I read *Ms.* magazine; listened to feminist and lesbian music I found at a local feminist bookstore and through flyers and local concerts; and watched some powerful documentaries, such as *Killing Us Softly: Advertising's Image of Women*. I saw more clearly how sexist, misogynist, racist, and homophobic our society was, how it encouraged people to see girls and women as sexual objects to be used, abused, and raped, and encouraged us to stay silent victims—from ads to TV, movies, mainstream music, and even some books.

I saw how it wasn't just the media that perpetuated these extremely unhealthy beliefs and behaviors. It was also regular people I came into contact with: the man who slid his hands over my shoulders and back when I was hugging my partner at Pride; the man who walked his dog with mine and others' every morning, who told me that he should have non-consensual sex (rape) with me to turn me heterosexual; the man who called out from his truck that I was beautiful and sexy and then idled there, as if I should take it as a compliment; the people who told me to smile, smile, smile...and so many more.

All those books, magazines, music, and films helped me see

that I wasn't alone, and that the rape, abuse, and harassment wasn't my fault. That change had to happen. And that I could be part of that change. So I went on rallies and marches with my partner—to Take Back the Night (which is anti-rape), International Women's Day, LGBTQIA (Lesbian/Gay/Bisexual/Transgender/Queer/Intersex/Allies) Pride, and Toronto's Dyke March, which I loved for how feminist it was. It felt (and still feels to me) like one of the best days of the year, since it's both political and a celebration, pushing back against oppression and taking back words that have been used to hurt us. I put my art in some art shows, such as one to commemorate the Montreal Massacre where fourteen women were murdered in a mass shooting at a Montreal university by a man because he thought they were feminists. I kept submitting my work to survivor newsletters. I started an abuse survivor support group at my high school, although only one other student attended because it's hard to talk about abuse when it's still happening. I sent my poetry and writing to a few publishers. I attended incest and rape survivor support groups, and connected with other survivors.

All of my ways of speaking out and being heard, of connecting to other survivors and feminists and the queer community and our allies, gave me back a piece of my soul that my abusers had stripped away. It strengthened me. The wounds to my soul are still there; they may never go away. But they were lightened by being heard, receiving compassion, and connecting to others—especially to my three closest friends who've become my family, and to two incredible therapists (one who was also a cult abuse survivor, who understood from experience what I'd been through and who had great compassion; and the other, who also has incredible warmth and empathy, gives me unconditional love, and has become like a mother to me). And I know from hearing from other survivors that my speaking out helped them, too, to know that they weren't alone. When you're in pain and you feel alone, your pain feels so much worse. But when you know others have gone through the same or similar experiences and have survived and even thrived, then you realize that you can, too. No matter what you've been through or how awful it's been, there are others out there who understand. You are not alone. And it will get better.

For me, my most powerful and healing way of being heard and helping others has been through my books. It took me more than ten years and hundreds of rejections by agents and editors to get my first novel, *Scars*, published—a book about a queer teen who was sexually abused and cut to cope, just as I had. I'd known I would face rejections, but as the years passed and they kept coming, I felt so desperate and depressed that I wanted to give up. I'm grateful now that I didn't. After *Scars* reached bookstores, reader letters poured in—and still keep pouring in—letting me know that my writing moved them; that they felt like I'd written about them, or that it helped them understand self-harm or sexual abuse or being queer; and that it helped them talk to someone for the first time, to stop cutting, and even to keep from killing themselves. For the first time I felt like I truly had a voice, and I continue to use that voice through writing and publishing more books, and interacting with my readers on social media. That is the power of speaking out: creating positive change and healing for others, as well as for ourselves.

I wasn't heard most of the years I was being raped, abused, and tortured; I certainly wasn't protected. But I think things are slowly changing, thanks to all the women (and men) who have spoken up and fought for change. In the US, Canada, the UK, and many other countries, men can no longer legally beat their wives or children; children are no longer forced to work in factories; and slavery is no longer legal. There are better laws to protect children and women from sexual abuse, rape, and harassment; better laws to protect the LGBTQ community from abuse and harassment; and more people are aware of the devastating effects of abuse, trauma, and sexual harassment. I think as a society we are moving toward greater compassion, awareness, and action, and toward abusers actually being held accountable, as seen by the #MeToo and #TimesUp movements. The internet has made a huge difference in bringing people together and making them aware of the systematic violence, misogyny, homophobia, and racism in our society. Now many children and adults are standing up against it and making themselves heard. I feel so hopeful about the #MeToo and #TimesUp movements (and so many others, such as #MarchForOur-Lives and #BlackLivesMatter), and the ways people are coming together to make positive change.

I believe that all these ways of speaking out—of saying #MeToo, you're not alone; I believe you and stand with you; #TimesUp and abusers need to be held accountable for their actions—help to make a real, positive, healing change in the world. I believe that we are more powerful together when we raise our voices, and that we have a greater chance now than ever of being heard. So I hope you'll speak out, too, in the ways that are safe for you to, and listen to others who are also speaking out. I want you to know that I hear you. I believe you. I want you to be safe, to work on getting safe if you're not, and to keep speaking out until you are heard. I want you to treat yourself gently and with love, the way you should always have been treated. I hope you follow your heart and your dreams, and don't let anyone crush them. I hope you keep the goodness, love, and hope in your soul, because they matter. You matter. Your dreams matter. And you are not alone. So keep speaking out, keep reaching out—and change will happen.

★ ★ ★ ★ ★

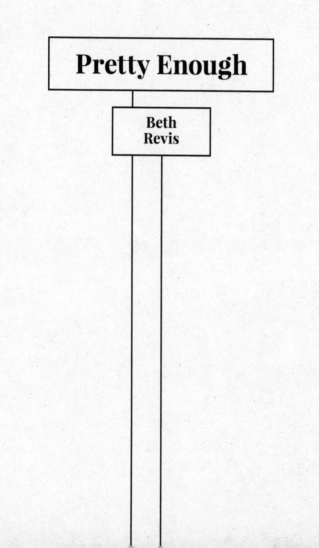

Pretty Enough

Beth
Revis

I was sixteen years old the first time a grown man told me I wasn't worth raping.

My friends and I were in a school play—*A Midsummer Night's Dream*—and my role was Anonymous Fairy #3. During break, we were allowed to walk to a convenience store a few blocks away to buy snacks and sodas, and we didn't bother changing out of our costumes. We wore bodysuits of flesh-colored material and lots of gauzy scarfs—there was the illusion of airiness, but everything was well hidden by the fabric.

One afternoon, three men were leaning on a truck outside of the store. We passed in front of them, and one of the men—a tall, scrawny guy probably my father's age—shouted at us. He had a bulge in his lower lip from a hunk of chewing tobacco, and when he grinned at us, his teeth were stained brown.

I don't remember what he said, exactly. It was something about our costumes, and the implication that we should take them off for him.

I'm from a small town, a very rural area. I had never had a man at least two decades older than me suggest anything sexual like that. I knew of catcalls from the way they were portrayed on television—a beautiful starlet whistled at by a crude construction worker who pushed his hard hat up his brow to better take a look at her legs. It was a joke in sitcoms. It was an opportunity for a hero to stick up for the girl. It was something the starlet easily brushed off.

But when it happened to me for the first time, it wasn't funny. No one stood up for me or my friends. And I didn't want to brush it off.

His words were loud and obscene. But it was his look—the way he seemed so *pleased* with himself—that infuriated me the most.

My best friend was with me, and I could tell the man's words bothered her—a lot. Had I been alone, I think I would have walked away, but instead, my protective instincts reared up. I whirled on the man, telling him to leave us alone.

He pushed himself off the side of the truck and lumbered over to me. He was at least a foot taller than me, and he used his height to his advantage. He peered down his nose, raking his eyes along my costumed body. Throughout the course of the play, I had thought the costume fun. We fluttered our scarves and danced around the stage, as free as the fairies we were pretending to be. But as this man looked at me, I wanted to hide. I felt ridiculous. I felt like a *thing*.

"I wasn't talking to *you*," he said with a sneer. "You're not pretty enough for me. I wouldn't touch you if they paid me."

His buddies all laughed, and I felt shame rise up in my cheeks. It was bad to be catcalled, yes, but somehow it felt worse to be pointedly told that the "compliments" weren't for me. That I was too ugly to be worthy of his unwanted touch.

I glanced back at my friend. She was tall and beautiful. She'd already had several boyfriends, and I hadn't. Boys told her she was pretty all the time. She was always the wanted one. I was not. So while I was all too familiar with the envy that often rose in my chest when I compared myself to her, I was woefully unprepared for that green-eyed snake to bite at me from the lips of someone else.

We left the men as they laughed at us, at *me*, at the way I was so easily silenced. I like to think I had some dignity in the way we walked away, but to be honest, I still think of that moment with shame. Twenty years later, I am certain that man has never once thought about that moment, except, perhaps, to chortle at me again. But I have never forgotten.

And I have never returned to that store. I quit getting candy and soda, and I found excuses to avoid walking that street with my friends. I completely altered my path to avoid the place of that burning shame.

He had taught me a lesson and taught it well: what happened to girls happened because of the way they looked. This was a lesson reinforced by people all around me, at every turn, even people I loved and respected. When there was news of a girl who'd been accosted, with her image in the paper, I saw the way people judged her and said that she shouldn't have been at that party, she shouldn't have been drunk, she was probably dressed like a slut. I wasn't invited to parties, I didn't drink to the point of drunkenness, and I tended to dress conservatively. A little part of my brain whispered in that man's voice: "It won't happen to you," and "Who would want you anyway?"

When I was out with guy friends, and they rated girls based on who they would tap and who they wouldn't, I was included in that conversation because I knew—and they knew, we *all* knew—that I was inherently never a part of the ranking. I wasn't even on their radar. I was "one of the guys," and I wasn't worth their rating. Ratings were for pretty girls. It never occurred to me how messed up such a ranking system was, and that no woman wants to be ranked based on those crude terms; I just knew that I was excluded, and it was because of my appearance. If the other girls were valued enough to rank, the fact that I wasn't merely added to the growing certainty deep inside me that I wasn't worth anything at all.

When I first became aware of the #MeToo movement, I read an article in which Uma Thurman discussed her encounter with an abuser. And while I wish I had been wise enough to truly understand the depth of her experience after reading it, I know in my heart that my first thought was, "Thank God I'm not pretty enough to be raped."

Then I immediately stepped back and thought, "No, that's not how that works. I *am* pretty enough to be raped."

I hope that you, unlike me, can see immediately how truly disturbed a way that is to think.

My knee-jerk reaction had been to put the onus of whether or not someone was harassed into terms of whether or not they were "worth" harassing. But I'm well educated, and I know women who have been raped. I understand on a fundamental level that rapists and harassers target women for a variety of reasons, and that I have as much a chance to be a victim as anyone else. I know that the blame doesn't lie in the way a woman looks, either physiologically or in her clothing. I know that there is no such thing as "pretty enough" to be raped or "ugly enough" to be saved.

And yet, when I was sixteen years old, a man at least two decades older than me told me I wasn't attractive enough to touch, and he laughed at me. He made me feel ashamed for not being objectified. He made me feel as if it were my fault that he was so rude. And so, two decades after that, the first thought I had when hearing a woman's story of being assaulted was, in a very sick and twisted way, gratitude for my ugliness.

I wish I could go back in time and tell sixteen-year-old me that it's not about attraction, prettiness, or even sex. That type of harassment comes down to power. That man had wanted to show his power over the girls he saw. He wanted to preen in front of his buddies. He wanted to pretend that young girls wanted him. And so he manipulated the situation into one where he had power. And when he didn't have power over my attraction, he shifted it to power over my self-worth.

I don't know if I would have believed myself then, but now, I know that's true. He proved he was powerful in the repercussions his comments had on my way of thinking. He influenced my perception of beauty and love and worth in ways that took decades to break. Just a few minutes, a handful of words—that was all it took. He was powerful…in that way.

But when I shift my perception, I see how weak he was. He had to belittle a child in order to make himself feel like a man. How utterly pathetic.

The #MeToo movement is about inclusivity—it's in the very words of the hashtag. *We are not alone.* It has never been a competition between the pretty girls and the ugly girls, even if some tried to pit us into that battle. How can there be a competition when those two sides—pretty and ugly—

don't even truly exist? We are each human individuals, un-able to be contained in one word, even if that is all some see. And while I spent a lot of my teenage years weighing myself on an invisible ranking system, believing my desirability was caught up in my appearance, believing my very worth was tied to the way others saw me…it is realizing that I am not alone that gives me back my power.

It is human nature to hold on to power once we have it.

I will do all I can to never let mine go again.

★ ★ ★ ★ ★

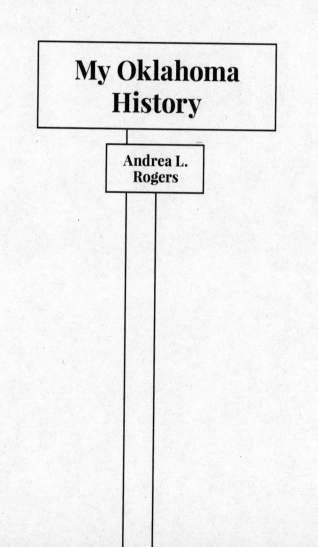

My Oklahoma History

Andrea L. Rogers

An Osage friend recently asked what I remember from my high school Oklahoma History course. Specifically, she asked if we learned about American Indian tribes and sovereignty. *Sovereignty* is a beautiful word. Sovereignty basically means federally recognized tribes have the right to govern themselves on their land. Tribal sovereignty is often threatened by federal and state governments, oil companies, and corporations. But sovereignty is also an adjective meaning "possessing supreme or ultimate power."

I like to think that women's power over their bodies is sovereign, though, like tribal sovereignty, this power is always threatened and threatening.

Until now, I haven't written about the time I was assaulted, at fifteen years old, at 2:00 in the afternoon in an empty high school classroom by a male student. I'll call him D. I prefer my pain with creative distance, when in fact I can draw a floor plan of the building we were in. It was a portable, a structure like a square, wooden mobile home, meant to be temporary, meant to hold the overflow of an unexpectedly large student body, but remaining for years before and after I graduated. I remember its sawdust smell and the joy of windows that opened in the fall and spring, even though there were no screens to keep out flies.

Some of the other concrete details are vague. What was I wearing that day? What was that cologne D always wore? Was he on the varsity football team that year?

I messaged a friend and asked her the varsity question. She retrieved her yearbooks and called me back.

"What's going on?"

"He assaulted me after class one day." For the first time, I told her the story. She had been my best friend in high school, and I had never told her.

"Why would he do that? He was good-looking. Girls liked him."

I didn't know what to say, though I was fairly sure I knew why he did it.

According to a policy report by the National Congress of the American Indian, three out of five American Indian and Alaska Native women experience sexual assault. Often this sexual violence goes unreported. One doesn't have to look far for the representation of Indian women and girls as sex objects. The Pocahottie Indian costume rears its faux buckskin shoulderless top every Halloween. Girls on social media look for likes as they channel their inner Indian Princess, their hair braided and accessorized with feathers and headdresses. Of the

Disney princesses, only Ariel, the mermaid, wears less clothing than Pocahontas, although Jasmine comes a close second.

In Tulsa, if you were brown and not African-American in 1985, it was assumed you were native. Yet I was the only obvious Indian in my Oklahoma History class. None of my friends were in there. Adults often don't get how important it is, the kind of protection a friend or two can provide in a hostile world. I'm a citizen of the Cherokee Nation of Oklahoma, and I had looked forward to learning Oklahoma's history, because I recognized how intertwined the history of Indian Territory was with federal Indian policy. The federal government promised in various treaties that Indian Territory would be an Indian nation for as long as the grass grew. Indian Territory was a geographic reality holding many separate sovereign Indian nations, while Oklahoma was a political reality. It is widely accepted that the name Oklahoma comes from a Choctaw word defining it as the home of the indigenous people. People who were forcibly relocated within its boundaries. But the things I learned in that class had nothing to do with our contemporary domestic dependent nations, the sovereign political entities that federally recognized tribes are today in Oklahoma. It was an exercise in nostalgia and propaganda and survivance.

Oklahoma History was taught by Coach in the period before he spent the rest of the afternoon in the locker room and on the football field. Coach was my favorite teacher—up until the day he ignored the boy assaulting me in his classroom.

The harassment started out low-key. D would come back from lunch and sit directly behind me. I felt him staring into the back of my head, but where else was he going to look? Coach was usually at his desk or a podium at the front of the room, directing us to take turns reading, teaching the his-

tory of the state, sometimes as if he actually cared about it. In
Oklahoma, history teachers are often hired for their ability
to coach, not their knowledge of history. Coaching experience was way more important than a history degree. Coach
got excited about history, though, sometimes speaking loudly
and pacing the room as if he was giving a sermon.

D would whisper things, and I would ignore him. When
Coach talked about the Trail of Tears, D whispered that his
grandma was also Indian. On more than one occasion, he
leaned his body forward across his desk and pulled his fingers through my long black hair. The first few times I forced
a laugh, as if it was a joke. I would say, "Stop," yanking my
head away. God forbid I be impolite, taking myself too seriously. But, eventually, I skipped right to angry. I even con-
templated cutting my hair.

In the years before removal and statehood, the Cherokee
tribe was a matrilineal culture. White men would marry into
the tribe, becoming a part of it, adopted through marriage to
a Cherokee woman. This allowed them to live and profit in
Indian Territory, but the women owned the property. They
could send their husbands away without negative repercussions if they no longer desired to be married. The children
belonged to the woman and her family. When Cherokee
traditional law was subverted by the federal government and
European-based laws, this would change. The families of suc-
cessful white traders became more patriarchal.[1]

Each day at the end of class, Coach said, "Put up the chairs,"
and walked out of the room to the restrooms attached to the
foyer between the other three classrooms in the building.
There were fewer students than chairs, so I would usually put

1   W. David Baird and Danney Goble, *Oklahoma: A History*. University of
Oklahoma Press, 2011.

up some of the extra ones. I was quiet and shy with teachers, so in place of words, I helped put away books or picked up classrooms. Often, I was the last person to leave the room.

According to Angie Debo's *And Still the Waters Run*, when the Chickasaw tried to pass laws protecting the tribe from the undue influence of white men on tribal affairs, "the white men held meetings and defiantly resolved that if any attempt were made to dispossess them they would 'exterminate every member of this council from the chief down.'"[2]

Aware of the potential of this threat, the Cherokees passed laws that determined marriage to a Cherokee woman would not confer property rights after 1877.[3] The Osage, too, were heavily impacted by the marriage of white men into the tribe. Several books detail the large-scale conspiracy to marry and then commit murder in order to siphon off the tribe's wealth. In Oklahoma, the possession of a native woman was often seen as a path to land ownership and money. Not so subtly, when President Theodore Roosevelt signed Oklahoma's statehood proclamation in Washington on November 16, 1907, it was celebrated at the same time in Guthrie, Oklahoma, by the symbolic marriage of an Indian woman (variously referred to as either Creek or Cherokee) called Miss Indian Territory to a man called Mr. Oklahoma.

I remember Coach talking about the mock marriage of the Twin Territories and the breaking up of tribal land by allotment to enrollees of the Choctaw, Cherokee, Chickasaw, Seminole, and Creek tribes. By the time I was in high school, though, my grandparents' allotments had been whittled down to a small percentage of what they had once been. An uncle

---

2   Angie Debo, *And Still the Waters Run: The Betrayal of the Five Civilized Tribes*. University of Oklahoma Press, 1989.

3   Ibid.

owned what little was left, acreage that held a family cemetery and my grandmother's empty house.

At the end of one class, I picked up textbooks left on the tables by the other students. They were clothbound, a dull brown with a gold embossed image of either a conquistador's helmet or a covered wagon. Both images are representative of invasion, not indigenous nations. Some copies were really old, some newer. It didn't matter, though, because the textbook hadn't been updated in years. I doubt the word *sovereignty* is in the index.

After I put away books, I put the chairs on the table upside down, so the custodians could sweep. I suddenly felt D behind me, pressing me into the table. I tried to turn and pull away, saying, "Stop it, D," but I was knocked backward onto the table. D's body was heavy on top of mine as he forced his hand under my sweater.

I screamed, "Get the fuck off of me! Goddammit!"

His shaved face pressed roughly against mine, while all hundred pounds of me kicked and shoved. It didn't move him an inch.

From the hallway, Coach hollered, "Who is cussing in my classroom?" His heavy footsteps preceded him. D stood back up, away from me. I rolled over and jumped up. I grabbed my books and ran out of the room, squeezing past Coach standing silently in the doorway.

I kept running. I didn't tell anyone. I didn't tell anyone for years. It is a shock when you find out others do not believe your body is your own. When leers and catcalls turn into grabbing and taking. You learn to be afraid of people.

I learned to always be afraid...

Sovereignty is the ability to govern yourself, the right to determine your own path. To be sovereign is to be independent. Treaties with Indian nations recognized their ability to govern themselves. It is an often-ignored fact that federally recognized tribes have the right to sovereignty. Human beings also have the right to their own body. That, too, is a threatened truth.

I don't know why a boy I hardly knew did what he did. The social conditions that create this kind of inhumane behavior—the expectation of access to a native woman's body—are both rudimentary and complicated.

Google "American Indian costume" for a sample of the way native women are seen. Look up information about Missing Murdered Indigenous Women and Girls. The disappeared and the dead haunt our native family trees. We share missing fliers on social media of American Indian and First Nations women and girls too often.

I don't know why my teacher ignored the scene in his classroom or what I expected him to do when he heard my screams. I do know that, after school, I went home and slept into the early morning the next day, because that was how I dealt with things I couldn't deal with. That's how I dealt with things I couldn't talk about, things that made my stomach hurt, things that terrified me, and things that made no sense.

I know I went back to class the next day—angry, but also frightened. I wondered what I did to deserve it. I didn't make eye contact with Coach or put away any books.

I was never again the last one to leave his classroom.

Since then, I have often heard people say you must forgive those who have harmed you in order to move on. I disagree. I don't believe you should forgive someone who isn't sorry. Forgiveness might be a response to the making of amends, but it is not something that should fill the absence of a violator's lack of regret.

The internal scars of the violation of a person's body sovereignty are often slow to heal. One of the first laws written down by the Cherokee responded to a first rape offense with whipping (fifty lashes) and the cropping of the left ear. The second offense earned one hundred lashes and the cropping of the right ear. A third offense was punished by death.[4]

Traditional Cherokee law was about maintaining balance in the world.

In *Fire and the Spirits: Cherokee Law from Clan to Court*, Rennard Strickland writes, the law "provided this seemingly barbaric revenge for what the Cherokees regarded as an even more barbarous crime."[5] To take away a person's power over their body, to allow this to happen without punishment, throws the world out of balance.

As a teacher, I have often asked my students, when I sensed something was wrong, if they felt unsafe. I see it as my job to help them navigate the world's dangers.

I wish my high school teacher had felt the same.

★ ★ ★ ★ ★

---

4   Rennard Strickland, *Fire and the Spirits: Cherokee Law from Clan to Court*. University of Oklahoma Press, 1975.

5   Ibid.

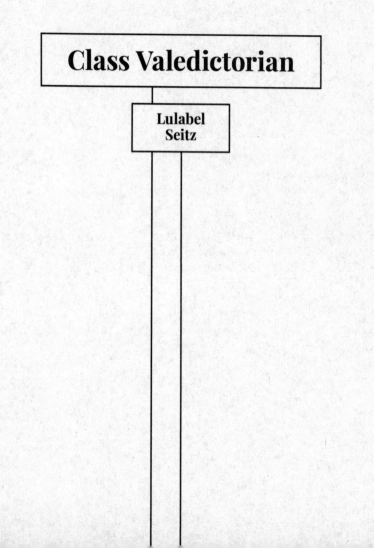

Class Valedictorian

Lulabel
Seitz

I was sexually assaulted my junior year of high school. After, people told me I didn't seem "the type" for this to happen to…but I guess there isn't really a "type," and it can happen to anyone.

I'm now going to Stanford, and have always tried to be an achiever, the highest in my high school class. I had several jobs and was always involved in activities. I went out a lot, had boyfriends, and made a game of how many yearbook signatures I could get. I guess people thought I was invincible.

For four years, I worked hard to be my school's valedictorian, and my efforts were rewarded senior year. Being valedictorian meant I got to make a speech (although my school principal tried to take that away, too). I wrote my speech carefully. I wanted to be optimistic, but to shed light on the adversity my class had to face to get to graduation.

I am not by any means the only person who was sexually assaulted or harassed at my high school. I believed that deserved to be talked about. My school officials warned me that I could not mention the issue of sexual assault in my valedictorian speech. Somehow, they caught word I was going to anyway. They pulled me out of class several times to tell me I was not allowed to.

But I knew what was right, and I knew what was wrong. I knew what many people had risked their lives for before me. I knew what countless wars were fought for. I knew what this country stood for.

Equality.

How can we have equality between men and women if we don't talk about the fact that men are allowed to harass and assault women?

I knew what I had to do.

So I took a breath while delivering my speech, and went off script to talk about this issue.

My school officials cut my microphone. I stood my ground. Most of my class cheered for me. Many gave me a standing ovation.

The press found the story, and the YouTube video of my uncensored speech went viral. There were articles about me in the *Washington Post*, *TIME* magazine, you name it. I never intended to do this for attention and fame, but I'm happy that this incident had such widespread attention. Because now, people *see*—they can't just shut women up. They can tell us to stop talking, and they can even cut our microphones, but they can't cut out our tongues.

Perhaps I was luckier than most people in my situation,

because with persistence, I was eventually heard. But I remember every word my perpetrator ever said to me; every compliment, and every insult. I remember the few good times, and the many bad times. I remember every time someone doubted me: a school official, a police officer, a friend, or a family member. But most of all, I remember how I found the courage to stand up, speak up, to say that this happened, and to say that it shouldn't happen anymore.

I don't enjoy going into the specifics of my story. It is not because I'm "triggered" or "ashamed," but because the specifics simply aren't relevant. The fact of the matter is that I was raped and otherwise sexually assaulted. The fact of the matter is that some high school athletes, empowered by popularity and trained by the aggression of their sports, quite often abuse the girls they date.

When I was a junior, my boyfriend, who was a senior at the time, broke up with me right before prom. As many high school girls would be, I was devastated. Then, one day I turned around in my AP English class and saw a new opportunity. A new source of hope.

It was him.

He was a big football player—a linebacker, he said. He had at least a foot and seventy pounds on me. He was popular but a bit of a loner, in a way that attracted me. He used to comment on the videos I would post of myself playing piano and seemed perfectly nice in every way. When we sat together during a guest speaker presentation, he looked at me slyly, a glimmer in his eyes letting me know he was interested. He stood up and shouted with his friends, which I later found was completely out of character for him, but a way to show off to me. We texted cute hearts and smiley faces. He asked me to a movie.

He wore a green polo shirt, met my dad, and seemed to be the picture of charm and kindness. Then my dad left.

He didn't talk to me much—not like he had over text, not like in our English class. It was like a switch flipped. He grabbed my hair and forced me to kiss him in the movie theater, even when I tried to push him off me. He called me a tease.

I felt bad and wanted to make it up to him. He said he'd give me the opportunity, and I started to go to his house during lunch breaks from school.

He was rich, and his house was a giant mansion that made me feel like a princess. Coming from a less well-off family, I had never seen such a giant and beautiful house in my life. He didn't seem to think it was anything special, though.

The story progresses from here as one may expect. He made me do things I didn't want to do. Eventually, I went on a school trip as captain of my school's Quiz Bowl team, which is basically like a more fun, academic version of *Jeopardy!* My friends and I ended up getting second place in the state of California in our competition. Empowered by this success, I decided I didn't really like this boy anymore.

Another boy asked me out on the trip, and I said yes.

When I came back from the trip, I walked into my English class holding a huge bouquet of flowers from another boy, hoping it would send some sort of message that I was taken, and I would finally be free of this superficially perfect, but abusive and unpleasant football player.

School ended and went into summer. I had two different internships with prestigious professors and a wonderful boyfriend. We used to go on fancy dinner dates on Friday nights and to the water park on weekends. Yet, every day, I still thought about that football player. Each day I reviewed the events that happened in my mind, asking myself why I was no longer with him. Asking myself what *I* had done wrong.

These flashbacks weren't pleasant, and were indicative of the lasting fear I had of this football player. Yet, when I broke up with my Quiz Bowl boyfriend at the beginning of our senior year (he didn't like the fact that I was smart, and I didn't like his attitude), I thought that these flashbacks about the football player were a sign of attraction rather than of fear and, frankly, PTSD.

One late night when I was still sad about my breakup, I texted the football player. It was innocuous. We decided we should hang out soon.

During lunch the following week, he picked me up again. We went to his house, hung out, and made out. Everything seemed fine, and I thought perhaps he had changed. I thought that since I was very clear and vocal about my dislike toward what he did last time around, things had changed.

Of course, he never changed. As young girls, we're always taught that we can change people, especially men. Belle in *Beauty and the Beast*, through her virtue and patience, was able to turn that disgusting, cursed beast into a chivalrous and handsome prince. In *Gone with the Wind*, the handsome profiteer Rhett Butler is willing to abandon his bad habits and affairs with prostitutes to be with Scarlett O'Hara. Most love stories are along these lines—not only is the woman *able* to change the man permanently and completely, but the man is *willing* to do so just to be with her.

Everything became worse and worse. He forced me to do a lot of things. He left bruises. He didn't stop when I said stop. We don't think that kids can act like this to each other, but he was seventeen, almost a man. Rape and domestic violence can be prevalent with kids that are still in school.

We all saw this coming; in hindsight, *I* saw this coming. After being beaten up in a car, being blackmailed, and hearing a rumor that my football player raped another girl at a party, I decided I'd had enough. I finally told my friends what happened, and they were appalled. They couldn't believe this was happening to someone they knew.

They helped me break up with the football player. We talked to him together, during a school break. He denied the threatening texts he'd sent me. Denied hurting me. He denied everything. No resolution was reached. So some of my friends went and told my school counselor.

At this point, I had been known only for being honest and a good student. Nobody had any reason to doubt me. And the counselors didn't—they took me seriously, and contacted the Title IX coordinator.

When someone is sexually assaulted or harassed in a high school, a person called the Title IX coordinator is in charge of doing everything possible to keep the victim safe. This may include reporting the incident to the police, suspending the perpetrator, organizing a restorative action plan, etc. This coordinator's literal *only* job is to protect the school from liability by protecting the complainant against the accused.

The Title IX coordinator for my school district was an old white man. In fact, he was the only one left of a generation of school officials who had all resigned, for unknown political reasons. I could instantly tell my fate was sealed. Good ol' boys protect good ol' boys. My perpetrator was going to stay in high school, consequence-free.

This was precisely what happened. The boy ended up confessing to some of his crimes, being arrested, and going to juvie for a night. Shortly after he was released from juvie, he was let back on campus, where he proceeded to spread lies about me and accuse me of forging his texts (of course, this was comical—I may be going to Stanford, but I don't have the slightest idea how to hack into Verizon Wireless servers to send fake texts from his number to myself).

Now I was angry. Both he and I had been voted "Most Likely to Take Over the World" in high school. It would be an understatement to say I had a reputation for being the opposite of a pushover.

I fought the school. I memorized Title IX and the California Educational Code. I cited every law, every piece of evidence, everything that would make it a necessity for school officials to discipline him or at the very least make him do independent study for the rest of the year. But who cares about a five-foot-four Asian girl citing the law, when the rich white football player's family hires a lawyer? They pretended to listen to me, and then they told me to be quiet. They told me I was on a "gag order."

They told me, no matter what I did, they couldn't do anything. They told me they would arrange it so he wasn't on campus when I was—which was only for four classes, because I took most of my courses at the community college—and that was it.

They said there wasn't enough evidence, even though I had text messages of the football player threatening me, and one of his past girlfriends came forward to say he blackmailed her to get sexual acts, too. His friends even said they didn't doubt that he did this to me. I found things he had written on the internet about a passion for violence and fantasies of abusing women. But none of this was enough. Not for these old white men. Words were less valuable than money.

In fact, a counselor told me that they were considering moving *me*, the valedictorian, student body treasurer, and jazz trumpet soloist, to the other local high school, so as to keep the peace between me and the football boy. They were going to move *me, against my will*, punishing me for his actions. I avoided this fate only by luck, because shortly after this, my Stanford acceptance letter arrived in the mail. The school wanted to take credit for my success, and they couldn't if they moved me to another school before graduation.

So, I lived out my senior year in fear. I still saw him around campus and heard rumors he had told people in the hallways. People became aware of what happened to me. I wrote a novel. I won a math contest. I traveled to Boston to visit the Massachusetts Institute of Technology, which I had also been accepted into. I dated a few people. On the outside, I seemed to be doing fine.

But inside me, there was a storm. I felt, more than ever, the injustice associated with being a minority woman. I felt, more than ever, that I was not being listened to because I didn't have enough money. I felt, more than ever, the need to *speak*: the need to break the forced silence. I felt like this was the new edition of the women's rights and civil rights movement. The discrimination wasn't so overt, but the message was the same: white men get away with what they want. The people in power are still mostly white men, too. And for the most part, they frankly don't give a damn. The problem is that we are not entirely out of our old system of patriarchy and white supremacy, even though a lot of times we act as though we are. So, we hold back on change, we don't listen to our rape victims, and we allow people to be in power who lack foresight and the understanding of all of this. We can't shed our implicit biases until we have lived in a system representing the positive change we seek for some time—a system that can't exist until we make the change.

Finally, time started to approach the moment I had been desperately waiting for: graduation. The moment we'd all been waiting for. I walked up to the podium to give my speech. I saw the football player in the audience, directly in front of me.

I gave my speech, and they cut my mike. I had originally planned to end with this message (which was later published in *Teen Vogue*):

Furthermore, it is truly the journey we took to get here that makes the Class of 2018 unlike its predecessors. The fires that put our daily lives on hold and took some of our homes—we didn't let that drag us down. When our teachers had to go on strike because they didn't receive the respect they deserve—we didn't let that drag us down. It helps that we had the support of compassionate and dedicated teachers, friends, parents, counselors, custodians, and librarians throughout the years. Learning on a campus in which some people defend perpetrators of sexual assault and silence their victims—we didn't let that drag us down. Even after four years of working our hardest and becoming the best class Petaluma High has ever seen, just to be told by those same some people that our love of learning, art, drama, music—anything—wasn't valuable enough to be funded, well we didn't let that drag us down, either. Time and time again, the Class of 2018 has demonstrated that although we may be a new generation, we are not too young to speak up, to dream, and to create tangible, positive change. As such, we will never be forgotten. How could we be?

The media storm happened after that. I was fortunate that many political, legal, and activist groups reached out to me, and I'm now working with stronger forces to stop this epidemic of sexual abuse. I am allowed to speak.

To the girls and boys who had this happen to you, too, whether you spoke up or not: know that what happened *did* happen. Know that your life is a lot worse now than it would have been if it didn't happen. But also know that bad people will get what's coming for them. Your perpetrator will not live a happy life. And he or she won't have a happy afterlife, either.

I'm not a victim because I'm not helpless. I stood up for myself and fixed the situation for myself, more or less without the help of others. I'm not a survivor, because I didn't survive some rare tragedy, and what happened to me is not something I'm proud or ashamed of. "Victim" and "survivor" imply that what happened changed my personality and became a part of who I am. It didn't. I experienced rape, sexual assault, and domestic violence. It is something that happened to me, yes. But now I move on. Now, I help to make sure that other people don't have to experience this, too.

★ ★ ★ ★ ★

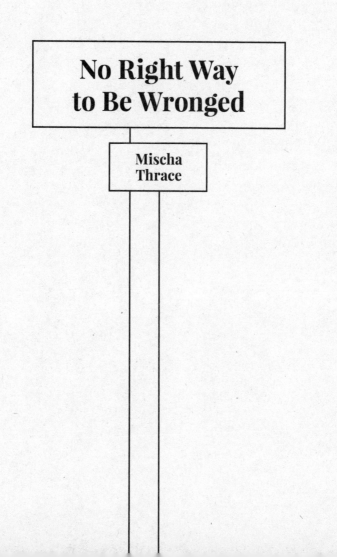

No Right Way
to Be Wronged

Mischa
Thrace

When people think of rape, they typically picture dark alleys full of armed assailants or drunk frat boys handing out red cups of spiked drinks. Their minds don't immediately leap to friends' bedrooms or the people they trust.

At least mine didn't, not until it was too late.

When I started college at sixteen, it was against the strident opposition of my high school and required special dispensation from the college to enroll without a diploma, but it was a move that saved my life.

When anyone asked why I made the leap, I said it was because I was bored, because the high school curriculum was beneath me, because I wanted to get on with my life.

And all of that was true, but it wasn't the whole truth.

I was good at hiding troublesome truths, even then, and

the whole truth was that I had become the designated weird kid in a school too small to escape such mantles. I was a horse girl, I was obsessed with forensic science before *CSI* made it cool, and I once made a poorly received joke about alien abduction that haunted my entire high school existence.

So, I left, and it was a revelation.

College was a haven for the outcasts, the passionate, the intellectuals. It was a space where I could create a version of myself that was divorced from the insecure, ostracized—and yes, bullied—girl I had been only months before. It was like being able to breathe for the first time.

I made friends. I joined causes and led protests. I found somewhere I fit, for the first time ever.

And the key to all that was Darren, who slotted right in as the Mulder to my Scully, which was what I'd wanted more than anything in the world.

I knew, even then, that I was weird in the wanting of this specific desire. While other girls my age were fantasizing about affairs with brooding stars and sweeping summer romances, I was looking for the sidekick. I wasn't interested in romance, I was interested in something better: genuine platonic love, in the truest sense of the word. I wanted the strength of Buffy and Xander, the chemistry of Donna and The Doctor, and the devotion of Harry and Hermione.

Darren seemed like a perfect fit for that. We were the geeks of the friend group, although admittedly, his brand of geek managed to look much cooler than mine. We took the same classes, could spend hours talking about how to save the world, and had an easy way of being with each other that made it hard to be apart.

Plus, I was secure in the knowledge that he had no sexual interest in *me*, because he was busy sleeping with everyone on campus, which I knew because he'd regale me with tales of his latest conquests over bowls of ice cream propped on the wall of pillows we built between us during our many movie marathons. I'd laugh and give him shit, all while secretly reveling in the fact that I got to be the best friend and not the booty call—because all those nights spent talking on the futon, bare feet propped on the cluttered glass coffee table, meant so much more than any fling ever could.

And then, after nearly two years of fast friendship, on a Friday night no different than the dozens of others we'd spent together, everything changed.

To this day, I want to blame it on something other than him. The shifting dynamic of our friend group, maybe—because by then, four of them had paired off into couples—or on my own naivete. I want to blame the pot he smoked before I got there, convince myself that it hijacked his brain, turned him temporarily into a monster.

I don't want it to be that he was just a shitty person who made a shitty decision.

But he was. And he did.

And it didn't matter that I cried, that I begged for him to stop; in less than ten minutes, he destroyed us.

And he didn't even care.

When I ran from his house that night, barefoot because it had taken too long to find one of my shoes, I didn't know what to do. I wasn't ready to go home, where my insomniac mother might hear me come in and want to chat, and I couldn't call anyone in our friend group—not yet. I wasn't ready to explain what had happened, because I barely understood it myself.

So, I drove for hours, until my heart stopped hammering and my hands were steady on the wheel, until I thought I could handle small talk if I was forced to, and only then did I let myself go home. If my mother heard me come in, she left me in peace. I showered and felt like a cliché, because I had read enough crime novels to know that's exactly what you're not supposed to do if you've been assaulted. But at the time, I couldn't make myself attach that concept to myself or, honestly, to Darren, so I washed away the evidence and went to bed.

I spent the rest of the weekend trying to forget. I didn't make any phone calls. I didn't tell a soul.

It never occurred to me to call the police or go to the hospital, because it wasn't like I'd been attacked by a knife-wielding stranger. I even started to question whether I'd been attacked at all. I was the one who'd shown up at his house like I'd been doing for months, completely of my own free will. I convinced myself that took away my right to call it what it was: rape.

During that first week back at school, he acted like nothing had happened. He was as cheerful and charming as ever, joking with professors after classes I could barely breathe in and joining our friend group for lunch. And when I saw that he was still being his lovable, charismatic self, I knew I never could call it what it was. No one would believe it. Hell, I barely believed it. Why would he ever force himself on me when he had so many girls already throwing themselves at him?

So, I told myself I was wrong, even though I shook when he sat down beside me in sociology. I told myself I misremembered the events of that night, even though the pressure on my chest said otherwise. I told myself it was my issue, my prudishness, my fault for being upset.

But I couldn't be near him anymore. I removed myself from the friend group, and they let me go, because no one wanted to deal with the constant rage-fest I'd become. I held on until the end of the semester, then transferred schools.

I thought this second change of schools would allow me another chance at transformation, but the anger continued to simmer like a living thing inside my skull, no matter how much I tried to divorce myself from its origin. It just became a part of who I was.

The logical thing would've been to get therapy, to talk to someone, but logic had left the building the moment I decided to never speak of that night.

So, I did the next best thing: I found people to hit.

Unlike most girls who take up martial arts in their late teens, I wasn't in it for fitness. I wasn't in it to meet a guy. I wasn't even in it for self-defense, because that horse had left the barn a long time ago.

I was in it for the violence, pure and simple.

Shallow as it may be, I refused to pick a system that was overly focused on philosophy. I knew many people considered that one of the great draws of martial arts, but I wasn't interested in belt testing or finding my inner chi. All I wanted was to pound the hell out of someone; I didn't have time to think deep thoughts about breaking their face.

With that criteria, I narrowed my options down to Krav Maga, Muay Thai, and mixed martial arts. Because Krav classes would require a ridiculous amount of travel and because I still wasn't sold on the whole college student by day, cage fighter by night vibe of MMA, I settled on Muay Thai, a form of kickboxing that allows knee and elbow strikes and seemed suitably violent.

There were two local places that offered Muay Thai classes, both mixed martial arts academies, and they appeared similar except in one regard—one offered a series of women-specific classes, while the other boasted an impressive roster of professional fighters, but didn't seem to cater to women at all.

The first gym, with their three-sessions-a-week women's program, ignored every one of my calls and let my messages go unreturned.

It was the best thing that could've happened.

When I called the second gym, the owner answered on the first try and made me feel totally at ease. I suddenly had no problem walking into a male-dominated, competitive fight gym. When I asked him if they offered classes for women, he laughed and said, "We don't separate women. There's no reason to. The classes are mixed level, and there'll be plenty of people to work with."

Despite the real desire to take up martial arts, I had to admit that part of me had gone in believing the stereotype that fighters were a bunch of meatheads or 'roid monsters, and that I would have to find women's classes if I wanted to train, but I couldn't have been more wrong. It turned out feminism was alive and well on the mat.

I was hooked from the first day. There's a school of thought that believes expressing anger is actually destructive to a person, but I found the opposite to be true. There is absolutely no better feeling than being allowed—no, *encouraged*—to hit things as hard as possible.

Those classes, sometimes as many as six a week, were better than any talk therapy could've been. The sweating and bruising and bleeding were cathartic in a way I couldn't have predicted. And somewhere between the endless hooks and jabs, I let the rage go. I didn't need it anymore.

The thing you learn around fighters is that they have heart. A kinder, better heart than most people would think. Fighters are people who get hit, who bleed, who get knocked out and never stop coming back for more. They know nothing if not perseverance. They understand pain and that it's just part of the game. You take hits, you might break, but eventually you heal.

You always heal.

I still carried my secret, but it wasn't a burden anymore. It didn't eat at me, it didn't define me.

But it didn't go away, not completely.

In 2018, I released my first novel, *My Whole Truth*, which, despite the title, was not based on a true story. Not exactly.

It was, however, a story about sexual assault and keeping secrets and staying silent.

So maybe a little bit based on a true story.

And those nuggets of truth were what made it so frustrating when a small group of early reviewers complained about my main character, Seelie. They said she wasn't pretty enough, she wasn't nice enough, but most vexingly, she wasn't vocal enough. These readers simply couldn't wrap their heads around why she—or anyone—wouldn't just tell the world about her assault, and I was surprised by how irrationally jealous I was of them. How nice must it be to never have had to keep a secret like Seelie's, to not understand why such a thing might feel necessary.

Those reviews worried me, though. Not because they were negative—no one likes every book they read, after all—but because what if those readers who were so exasperated with Seelie's silence had someone in their own lives grappling with a difficult secret? How might their judgment be hurting the people they loved, silencing them further?

But even as I wrote it, I should have known that letting Seelie control her secret wouldn't go over well with everyone. We live in a world that thinks it's owed our stories and demands our secrets, merely by virtue of their existence, and expects victims to scream their pain from the rooftops so everyone can Tweet about it in real time.

It seems that there has become a "right way" to be wronged: be a pretty, white, cis-het female; be affected, but not broken; be pissed, but not too pissed; and always be ready to be a spokesperson for a group you never wanted to be part of.

Now, this isn't to say that the spotlight on trauma is a bad thing, not at all. In fact, it's vital if we want to have better laws and a safer world. The #MeToo movement in particular has done incredible work in altering how we talk about sexual assault and has changed the very landscape of sexual politics.

However.

For every person who publicly shares their story, there are countless more who can say "me too" only in their heads, who aren't ready to tell the world their truth, or who just want to leave it behind. And that's okay. There is no single right way to be a victim.

I let Seelie keep her secret because I got to keep mine, because I know what it's like for those who remain silent, who lash out, who make mistakes. I understand those who can't tell their closest friends the things that haunt them, never mind the world. And I empathize with those who question whether they even have a story to tell, because I know that if they have to ask, they probably do. The aftermath of assault isn't pretty or logical or even remotely consistent, so to expect all victims, whether real or fictional, to respond in a certain way is unrealistic.

Plus, the silence isn't always forever.

But it's okay if it is.

★ ★ ★ ★ ★

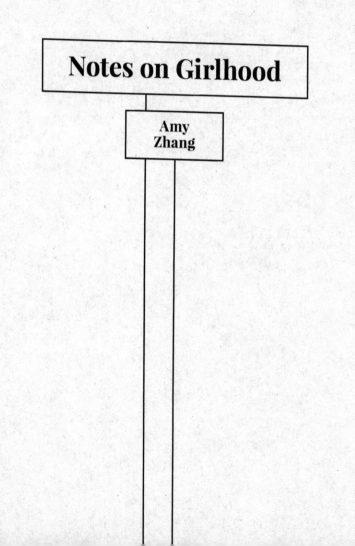

Notes on Girlhood

Amy Zhang

At fifteen, I wrote my first book, because every feeling was overwhelming. Every awkwardness was unbearable. I was sure I felt things more deeply and more vividly than other people. I felt emotion spilling out my seams.

After the first time I had sex, I wrote a letter to myself.

It was a bad letter. I was full of feeling, bursting with it. After all, it was about sex for the very first time. My head was spinning with a thousand fresh vulnerabilities.

Over the years I've tried many versions of this letter, at worse or better times. So here it goes: once more, with feeling.

As a little girl, I wanted to teleport. I thought it was a solid, clever wish, if ever I were to meet a genie or a properly functioning wishing well. I could travel all over the world but come home to my own bed every night. I could go wherever I wanted and leave whenever I wanted. I could always return somewhere more familiar, more comfortable. I imagine a lot of children feel this way, which is why there's a home base in tag.

"I'm home!" you scream, fleeing from someone fast on your heels. "I'm safe!" *Safe* is where no one has power over you. *Home* is all yours.

The thing about girlhood is that you also learn a lot of anxiety. In the wishing well, you splash your hem and someone—an adult, an authority—tells you it's not ladylike. And so you panic—what's *ladylike*? What disqualifies? Getting wet, making a wish? The truth is *ladylike* falls in the ambiguous lexicon of punch vocabulary that accosts all children, among things like *kind* and *polite* and *good*. What is it to be kind? To be polite, to be good? I'm not saying we don't teach boys to be kind and polite and good, because of course we do. But maybe we remind girls a little more. Maybe we admonish them more often. Maybe we learn a little more anxiety, and it's a little too much. After all, anxiety comes when you are uncertain, and when you are experiencing so many things for the first time, uncertainty is inevitable.

Anxiety is lonely; an infectious thing, it tinges every experience.

But being little is also wondrous. Almost everything you experience is brand-new. Then you get older, gather a little more context. You feel a sensation again and again, until it's familiar, until there are patterns in what brings it about.

This one is *awe*: I feel it when music soars or when the sky is particularly extraordinary. This one is *confidence*: I feel it when all my friends laugh at my joke. This one is *loneliness*:

I feel it when I can't communicate well. I am stuck in my body, and you in yours.

The first time I had sex I felt lonely. Also wildly confused. Also giddy, flattered, a little thrilled. But mostly I felt lonely.

It's not ladylike to talk about sex. I had the feeling it wasn't polite or good, either, though I didn't know why. What I learned about sex was not to have it. It made me anxious to ask why, so the narrative comes incomplete. Eventually I understood that I would bleed or maybe not bleed, that maybe it would hurt when the hymen tore or maybe it wouldn't, that it was supposed to be fun but sometimes it wasn't. All by euphemism, none with certainty.

So when I was having sex for the first time, I didn't know how to tell him that what he was doing didn't feel good, but that other thing he stopped doing *did* feel good, because I wasn't sure what I was allowed to feel during sex at all. Also, when you're feeling something for the first time, it's hard to say whether you liked it or not. It all happens too quickly to tell. I was uncertain, and then I was panicked with uncertainty. I didn't know how to talk about it. It felt silly to ask. And then I was lonely, and then it was over.

Having sex is a difficult thing. No one acts like it, but it is. There are all sorts of prerequisites to pleasure. You see anatomy you're unfamiliar with and you're expected to know just what to do, even though all bodies are different, and understand different experiences as *good*. This person likes attention to their neck and lips, this person doesn't. This person thinks tenderness feels good, this person thinks tenderness feels too vulnerable to qualify. Sex is difficult in the way that friendship or art is difficult. It's not straightforward or altogether consistent, and requires a great deal of forethought for someone else. It takes real work.

It took me a while to understand this. In the meantime, the sex got worse.

I was with a man, and he hurt me. He assaulted me. And it changed me.

What happened was that he got angry and slammed me against the bed with his hands around my neck. It was the densest shame I have ever felt. It was consuming, like it was the only thing I had ever known. It felt like a circuit between the amygdala and hypothalamus, communicating fear and releasing a flood of hormones in response. In fearful moments, steroids come to aid the body for fight or flight, but impair rational thought. There is no logical response—or rather, the brain cannot respond logically. It's flooded. What do the brain's natural opiates feel like? What do steroids, what do catecholamines, what do corticosteroids? They feel like static, like when your foot falls asleep; but instead the sensation is in your forehead, the back of your neck, the palms of your hands, so that it's difficult to move around them and think, rationally, *If he hurts me, then I should leave.* It feels like you're going to die, in the sense that the next day becomes inconceivable, and also in the sense that he might kill you by accident because you are so small, and so uncertain.

What I felt that night, for the first time, was the weight of a person who wanted to wound me. I'd never experienced it so intimately, in such a physical way. Everyone who has been prodded to tears by a playground bully knows the particular vulnerability and shame of facing someone who is thrilled, in some way, by pain. But this was different. I was naked, and I was not having fun anymore.

★ ★ ★

A list of things ruined for me after the assault: banana nut muffins, a certain movie, a certain place, a nameless cologne. This is a viscerally painful list. It makes my chest seize, my throat, my arms. *I don't want to be here. I don't want to feel this.* That's what a trigger is, like teleporting to the worst day of your life. Over and over. Dragged back too quickly to think, *No, stop, I don't want to.* All of a sudden you are flushed with feeling, and the feeling is terrible and everywhere.

After the assault, I spent a lot of time thinking about what happened, and how it could have happened and why it happened to me. All my life I thought nothing terrible could happen to me, because nothing terrible ever had. After, everything was a trigger. Everything made the hormone response kick back in. I thought about it all the time, the way you can't help poking a canker sore with your tongue, even after your face screws up with hurt.

I thought, *I had a bad feeling about him, but I went home with him anyway.*

I thought, *I saw him more than once, and I shouldn't have.*

I thought, *I am so stupid.*

I thought, *How could I be so stupid?*

There is a peculiar, untouchable shame after assault. It's like laying an open hand on a hot stove. When you flinch away, it's a visceral feeling; except of course you cannot flinch away from yourself, the feelings in your body, the memory in your head. I had known he was a bad guy. He made me count my calories, which is totally a bad guy thing. And yet. And yet.

The worst shame was this: after he hurt me, I was stunned. I felt nothing at all. He was so sorry that he began to cry as I sat up, and then I *did* feel something else. I wanted to laugh. But he was sorry, and it was unkind to refuse an apology. I'd known that since I was a little girl, and right then it felt like the only thing I knew for sure.

So I took him into my arms. I told him it was okay. No harm done.

This particular shame took the longest for me to grapple with. Even after I was able to comprehend that my naivete was not to blame for someone else's predatory inclinations, I was still ashamed of my compassion. I had been sorry that he was sorry; I was so sorry I held him after he hurt me. It was an incomprehensible, dissonant thing.

And then I was devastated. I don't know quite how to tell you about that particular experience of devastation. Everything was terrible. The feelings that overwhelmed me were not *awe* or *beauty*, the good kind of thrill. Mostly I was tired. I was horribly uncomfortable in my body. It was exhausting to dress it, to move it through proper conversations, to be authentic. All my life, I had thought of myself in terms like *kind* and *polite* and *good*. But I was not certain anymore that any of them were beneficial traits for a woman in this world. So I did not feel like myself, which begs the question: Who did I feel like?

This is why it's difficult to navigate around trauma. Suddenly everything is ambiguous, most of all yourself.

This tends to make sex much worse. It seems obvious now that bad sex is not worth having, but the sort of shame I felt was only manageable if I decided sex wasn't a big deal. If sex wasn't a big deal, then neither were its consequences. If sex wasn't a big deal, if instead it was somehow funny or absurd or easy, I could stop being devastated. So I started showing up to brunch with stories: *I hooked up with someone last night.* What I meant was, *I let a man fuck me last night and felt power-*

ful because I refuse to hurt over it, which is easier than *I let this happen to me. I did this to my body.*

The spoiler is that after this whole episode, I went to therapy twice a week for two years, because obviously this is a setup for terrible, upsetting sex. I cried after every single sexual encounter I had. A catcall could set me sobbing. I didn't want anyone to look at me. I didn't want to be seen.

A curious thing: I wasn't the only one. Other friends came with stories we brushed off as funny, even though they were wrought with false notes. We brandished bruised hips and blacked-out nights. Our pain was already normalized—in porn, by experience. It feels, again and again, like there are too many problems in our way. There are problems of gender and power. There are problems of empathy. There are countless societal landmines.

I'm not sure how to write about getting through it, except to say that I did. I went to therapy. I had good friends, and we learned from each other. I took some time to figure out what I wanted and how to feel okay about asking for it. It's still an ongoing process, but it feels better acknowledged than it did when I left it to fester.

How does assault happen? I think because most of us have no idea how to have sex when we first decide we want to, and then we learn at all different paces. The stakes are high. The mistakes are often unbearable.

Assault happens because assaulters are too deep inside their own heads. I don't say this with sympathy for offenders, but I do think that the phenomenon of being so focused on your own experience that you disregard your partner's pain speaks to a societal pathology. In girls, we fetishize uncertainty when it comes to sex. Somehow it's still sort of expected for a girl to be inexperienced, and thus unsure of what she wants or likes. Then there's pressure on both parties to push past, to pretend to know what you're doing. Fear is silly and childish. Anxiety kills the mood, which feels like the biggest faux pas of all.

It feels useless to say that we should be kinder people. Worse, it feels naive, and I've explained the problem of naivete. But it seems to me that we don't have a stable cultural practice of empathy during sex—far less than we do in our friendships, or even in our art. The bar should be higher, and we should want to clear it with quite a lot of room. I'm not sure what the solution is, or even the whole problem. I don't think that's the point of this essay.

Mostly I'm trying to explain something to myself. I'm afraid of sounding angry. Each time I try to write, I feel like my insides have been clawed out through my mouth. I think I want to say something profound about how consent is far more difficult than we pretend it is, and that we must reframe the way we look at sex so it's not. The delivery is trickier. Each time I try to write about this, I am flustered and stunned again. I am squirming in my skin. Sometimes the feeling is like quicksand, and all of a sudden I'm frantic to leave it and mired in confusion. Sometimes I feel despicable with wounds, and then I feel boring. There are things still too difficult to think about, much less write down. Of course, that's the whole problem.

Instead, let's talk about good sex. Assault is not sex, in the way that bullying is not friendship. Good sex isn't lonely, or wordless, or out of reach. It's really pretty simple. It is, *This is what I like*. It is, *Does this feel good?* More concrete things. Masturbation is vital. When you're feeling a certain pleasure for the first time, it's going to overwhelm. Reciprocation becomes difficult; so, probably, it's a good idea to orgasm on your own before you expect yourself to help someone else. Good sex is comfortable, and comfort comes with familiarity. Before you have sex, you must be able to say no to sex, which sounds obvious, but once felt impossible to me. What is the goal of sex, anyway? Certainly not to keep up an image of being easygoing, down for anything, spontaneous. It just seemed much more manageable to be uncomfortable than to cause someone else discomfort, but it turns out we should all be comfortable in the first place. It seems awfully suspicious that this was not made clear to me from the beginning, but that blame falls on all of us, as does the responsibility to do better.

For a long time, I carried this awful shame for an innocence that someone else took advantage of. It feels good to recognize this. When I wrote letters to younger selves, I was appealing to this naivete, like it was something to be intercepted before it could do more harm. But of course it wasn't the innocence that was causing me harm—it was the men who were harming me, and the world that allowed them to. There's no shame in inexperience, but there's loads in taking advantage of it.

I still have a lot of feelings. But fewer are incomprehensible. It's easier to recognize when I'm overwhelmed, and to identify the sorts of things that overwhelm me. It took me a while to feel steady in my body again, but I did. I do. I know a good deal more about myself than I did then. The partners I choose do, too. For now, this must suffice.

★ ★ ★ ★ ★

Resources

If you have experienced harassment or abuse, you may have found triggers in these pages. Rape. Incest. Exploitation. The #MeToo stories shared here are hard, but there are people and organizations out there who care and want to help. Please use the resources below if any of these stories upset you, or if you've had similar experiences. Please reach out if you need support.

TEEN LINE
teenlineonline.org
1-800-TLC-TEEN (852-8336)

Kids Help Phone (Canada)
kidshelpphone.ca
1-800-668-6868

Kids Help Line (Australia)
kidshelpline.com.au
1-800-55-1800

LGBT National Youth Talkline
www.glnh.org
1-800-246-PRIDE (7743)

The Trevor Project
www.thetrevorproject.org
1-866-488-7386

The Childhelp National Child Abuse Hotline
www.childhelp.org/hotline
1-800-422-4453

Didi Hirsch's Suicide Prevention Crisis Line
didihirsch.org/services/suicide-prevention/crisis-services
1-800-273-8255

RAINN (Rape, Abuse & Incest National Network)
www.rainn.org
1-800-656-HOPE (4673)

WAVAW Rape Crisis Center (Canada)
www.wavaw.ca
1-877-392-7583

About the Authors

Patty Blount grew up quiet and invisible in Queens, New York, but found her superpower writing smart and strong characters willing to fight for what's right. Today, she's the award-winning author of edgy, emotional contemporary romance. Powered by way too much chocolate, Blount gives a voice to characters society would much rather ignore—characters facing situations like rape (*Some Boys*, 2014; *Someone I Used to Know*, 2018), bullying (*Send*, 2012), and grief (*Nothing Left to Burn*, 2015). She enjoys hearing from her readers, so visit her website or follow her on Twitter, Facebook, or Instagram.

Jennifer Brown is the author of the young adult novels *Bitter End*, *Perfect Escape*, *Thousand Words*, and *Torn Away*, as well as the Shade Me series. Her debut young adult novel, *Hate List*, was chosen as an ALA Best Book for Young Adults, a *VOYA* Perfect Ten, and a *School Library Journal* Best Book of the Year. She lives in the Kansas City, Missouri, area with her husband and children. You can visit her online at www.jenniferbrownauthor.com.

Born in San Diego, California, **Tiffany Brownlee** is a graduate of Xavier University of Louisiana, working as a middle school English teacher in the New Orleans area. Her debut novel, *Wrong in All the Right Ways*, a YA retelling of Emily Brontë's *Wuthering Heights*, was published in July 2018. When she's not writing, she can be found in a ballet dance studio working on her pointe technique, in a bookstore buying (and reading) more books than her house has space for, or in any restaurant where they sell her favorite food: fish tacos.

Jess Capelle writes suspenseful stories with complicated girls. Sometimes she throws zombies in the mix. A native Texan, Capelle lives in Houston with boy cats who like to "help" with her work. You can find her writing online at places like The Hanging Garden and Eye to the Telescope. A complete list of her published work is available on her website, www.jesscapelle.com.

Kenna Clifford is a filmmaker and student currently living in British Columbia. She graduated high school in 2018 and is currently working on a fine arts degree, as well as a myriad of short film and writing projects. She awaits the day when she'll have a lot more to put into the bio sections of her (hopefully many) published works and IMDB pages.

Eva Darrows is the pseudonym for *New York Times* bestselling author Hillary Monahan, author of *Mary: The Summoning* and

Mary: Unleashed, and, as Eva Darrows, the critically acclaimed *The Awesome*. Darrows lives in Massachusetts with her family of some parts human, more parts fur kids.

Dana L. Davis is an author and actress who lives and works in Los Angeles. Her debut novel, *Tiffany Sly Lives Here Now*, was nominated for YALSA's 2019 Quick Picks for Reluctant Readers. Her second novel, *The Voice in my Head*, was published in May 2019 by Inkyard Press (formerly Harlequin TEEN). She has starred in *Heroes*, *Prom Night*, *Franklin & Bash*, and *10 Things I Hate About You*. Davis is a classically trained violist and the founder of the Los Angeles–based nonprofit Culture for Kids LA, which provides inner-city children with free tickets and transportation to attend performing-arts shows around LA County. She currently stars in the following animated series: *Star vs. the Forces of Evil*, *Craig of the Creek*, and *She-Ra*.

Ronni Davis grew up in Cleveland, Ohio, where she tried her best to fit in—and failed miserably. After graduating from The Ohio State University with a BA in Psychology, she worked in insurance, started a family, taught yoga, and became a cat mom. Now she lives in Chicago, where by day she copyedits everything from TV commercials to billboards, and by night she writes contemporary teen novels about brown girls falling in love. When she's not writing, you can catch her playing the Sims, eating too much candy, or planning her next trip to Disney World.

Natasha Deen loves stories—exciting ones, scary ones, and especially funny ones! As a kid of two countries (Guyana and Canada), she feels especially lucky because she gets a double dose of stories. Her recent books include *In the Key of Nira Ghani*, *Lark and the Dessert Disaster*, and *Thicker than Water*. When she's not working on her manuscripts or visiting schools, she spends a lot of time trying to convince her dog and cats that she's the boss of the house! You can visit her at www.natashadeen.com and follow her @natasha_deen on Twitter and Instagram.

Nicolas DiDomizio writes contemporary fiction for teens and adults. His debut novel, *BURN IT THE F*** DOWN*, is forthcoming from Little, Brown. He lives in New Jersey with his boyfriend and their bulldog.

Namina Forna is a screenwriter based in LA and the author of *The Gilded Ones* (2020), an upcoming YA fantasy trilogy. She has an MFA in film and TV production from the University of Southern California School of Cinematic Arts and a BA in English from Spelman College, and is committed to telling whimsical, fantastic, and unexpected stories for teens.

Jenna Glass wrote her first book—an "autobiography"—when she was in the fifth grade. She began writing in earnest while in college and proceeded to collect a dizzying array of rejections for her first seventeen novels. Nevertheless, she persisted, and her eighteenth novel became her first commercial sale. Within a few years, Glass became a full-time writer, and she has never looked back. She has now published more than twenty novels under various names.

Janet Gurtler has written over twenty books for teens and kids. Her teen books have been Junior Library Guild selections and recognized as Best Books for Teens by the Canadian Children's Book Centre. She lives just outside the Rocky Mountains and is so Canadian, she apologizes when people bump into her.

Teri Hall is unapologetically breathing, despite life's challenges. She is the author of a YA dystopian trilogy comprising *The Line*, *Away*, and *The Island*, as well the adult novel *New Zapata*, which is about what happens when Texas secedes from America (as it has actually done once already) and bans abortion and divorce. She has written three novels under the pseudonym of Jack Blaine, including *Helper12* and *Twitch*, which she describes as frothy sci-fi romances. She is currently revising her eighth novel, *Murmurations*, which is her favorite so far.

Ellen Hopkins is the *New York Times* bestselling author of fifteen young adult novels and four novels for adult readers. She lives in Carson City, Nevada, with her extended family. Hopkins considers it a gift and an honor that her Facebook, Twitter, Tumblr, and Instagram pages get thousands of hits from teens who claim Hopkins is the "only one who understands me." Find her at www.ellenhopkins.com, where you can also find links to her social media pages.

Mackenzi Lee holds a BA in history and an MFA in creative writing from Simmons College. She is the *New York Times* bestselling author of the historical fantasy novels *This Monstrous Thing*; *The Gentleman's Guide to Vice and Virtue*, which won a 2018 Stonewall Honor Award and the New England Book Award; its sequel, *The Lady's Guide to Petticoats and Piracy*; and *Semper Augustus*. She is also the author of *Bygone Badass Broads*, a collection of short biographies of amazing women from history you probably don't know about (but definitely should), based on her popular Twitter series of the same name. When not writing, she works as an independent bookseller, drinks too much Diet Coke, and romps with her Saint Bernard, Queenie.

Saundra Mitchell is an Edgar-nominated YA author, and she has been a phone psychic, a car salesperson, a denture deliverer, and a layout waxer. She's dodged trains, endured basic training, and hitchhiked from Montana to California. The author of more than fifteen books for tweens and teens, Mitchell's work includes *Shadowed Summer*, The Vespertine series, *All the Things We Do in the Dark*, and editing three anthologies for teens, including *All Out* and *Out Now*. She always picks truth; dares are too easy. Visit her online at www.saundramitchell.com or @SaundraMitchell on Twitter.

Ali Novak is a Wisconsin native and graduate of the University of Wisconsin-Madison's creative writing program. She started writing her debut novel, *My Life with the Walter Boys,* when she was only fifteen. Since then, her work has received more than 150 million hits online. When she isn't writing, Novak enjoys Netflix marathons; traveling with her husband, Jared; and reading any type of fantasy novel she can get her hands on. You can follow her on Wattpad, Facebook, Twitter, and Instagram @fallzswimmer.

Since earning degrees in Biology and Psychology from the University of California Los Angeles, **Eve Porinchak** has lived all over the planet and spent much of her time in and out of jail—as a creative writing teacher for teen inmates. A former agent with Jill Corcoran Literary Agency, she also attended medical school, served as a social worker with foster youth and homeless populations, and taught everything from first grade to college courses. Porinchak writes stories featuring youth she feels have been underrepresented in children's literature, such as those born into gang life, the abandoned, and the incarcerated, who—ironically—have the most fascinating tales to tell. Her first book, the critically acclaimed *One Cut*, a haunting nonfiction story with a juvenile justice bent, launched Simon and Schuster's young adult true crime line Simon True in 2017.

Cheryl Rainfield is the award-winning author of *Scars*, about a queer teen survivor who must face her past and stop hurting herself before it's too late; *Hunted*, about a teen telepath in a world where any paranormal power is illegal; and *Stained*, about a teen who is abducted and must rescue herself. Rainfield is a lesbian feminist, incest and torture survivor, and an avid reader and writer. She lives in Toronto with her little dog, Petal, and is working on new novels for teens. You can find her on her website, CherylRainfield.com, or on Twitter, Instagram, and Facebook @CherylRainfield.

Beth Revis is a *New York Times* bestselling author with books available in more than twenty languages. Her debut title, *Across the Universe*, kicked off a career in science fiction, but Revis has also published fantasy with *Give the Dark My Love*, contemporary with *A World Without You*, and nonfiction with the Paper Hearts series, which aids aspiring writers. A native of North Carolina, Revis is currently working on a new novel for teens. She lives in rural North Carolina with her boys: one husband, one son, and two massive dogs.

Andrea L. Rogers is a citizen of the Cherokee Nation of Oklahoma and a graduate of the low-res program at the Institute for

American Indian Arts. She grew up in Tulsa, Oklahoma, but currently lives in Fort Worth, Texas, where she is a teacher at an all-girls public school and the mom of three daughters. At IAIA, she was mentored by several strong indigenous writers and teachers. While there, she completed her short story collection, *Man Made Monsters*, a meditation on love, loneliness, family, and the monsters in society that walk with us. Native people are centered in this collection, along with a cast of vampires, werewolves, zombies, aliens, ghosts, two handsome princes, and a Goatboy. Her short stories have been published in *Transmotion*, *Kweli Journal*, *Yellow Medicine Review*, and *The Santa Fe Literary Review*. Her children's book with Capstone, *Mary and the Trail of Tears: A Cherokee Removal Survival Story*, comes out in 2020.

Lulabel Seitz is currently a student at Stanford University, double majoring in applied mathematics and economics. She aspires to someday be a professor of upper division mathematics and to do math-based economics research. Her story went viral internationally when she mentioned the issue of sexual assault in her high school valedictorian speech, and subsequently caused a freedom of speech–related protest at her graduation.

Mischa Thrace has worked as an English teacher, a horse trainer, a baker, and a librarian, and has amassed enough random skills to survive most apocalypses. She lives in Middle-of-Nowhere, Massachusetts, with her husband and their one-eyed wonder dog. She loves tea, all things geek, and not getting ax-murdered during long walks in the woods.

Amy Zhang is the author of *Falling Into Place* and *This Is Where the World Ends*. She currently lives in New York with her best friend and a foster pup.